Conflict Resolution

Julia Jasmine, M.A.

Teacher Created Materials, Inc.

Cover Design by Darlene Spivak

Made in U.S.A.

ISBN 1-57690-125-4

Order Number TCM 125

Table of Contents

Introduction

There is much more to conflict resolution than just learning a few techniques for resolving conflicts. In order for me, for example, to get to the point where I can—with any degree of effectiveness— learn, use, and then teach the skills necessary for resolving conflicts, I must know who I am (develop self-concepts), know who others are (grow in social awareness), know how to exchange ideas (acquire communication skills), and figure out why I should care enough to do all of this (develop respect and empathy).

It would also help a great deal to know how to differentiate between such abstract concepts as cooperation and competition, rules and self-direction, equal treatment and special circumstances, and justice and compassion. It would be even better if I could then choose the appropriate response for a given situation and offer some kind of logical or emotional rationale for my choice.

As I go through these steps, I must lead my students through them also. Then both they and I can begin to use, with some promise of success, the actual tools for resolving conflicts: assertiveness, negotiation, compromise, and mediation.

In this book you will find some basic directions for laying these successive tiers of indispensable foundation work as well as ways to construct the system you will use for resolving conflicts. A welcome bonus of this approach is that many conflicts disappear altogether in the process and many of those that remain become less significant or, at least, less threatening.

Developing Self-Concept

The Bottom Line

The development of self-concept is the bottom line in building a strategy for conflict resolution. Until students have a fairly realistic picture of who they are, they cannot deal effectively with the world around them. The details of this picture will vary, of course, becoming appropriately more complex according to the ages of the students involved, but the basic components will stay pretty much the same.

Webster's (1994) equates self-concept with self-image: one's idea of oneself and one's own **identity**, **abilities**, and **worth**. Although the development of self-concepts is often thought of as synonymous with the development of self-esteem, self-esteem is actually only a part of the broader definition of self-concept and, as a perception of worth, is usually dependent upon the way people perceive their identities and abilities. The self-concepts that people form are necessarily subjective, although they can be corrected and modified by periodic reality checks and extrinsic interpretations, and the development of self-esteem is the final personal spin applied to an already individual process.

> **Until students have a fairly realistic picture of who they are, they cannot deal effectively with the world around them.**

Let's Look at Identity

Identity is the first of the three components of self-image or self-concepts that will be considered here.

A Confusing Idea

Identity can become a confusing idea simply because it can be defined in two totally disparate ways: the condition or fact of being the same or exactly alike (sameness, oneness) and the condition or fact of being a specific person or thing (individually). (Webster, 1994) Most people establish their identity using both of these approaches simultaneously. They decide on the group that they belong to, or identify with, and then they decide on the qualities that make them individuals within that group.

Identity with a Group

One might decide on one's group based on criteria such as gender, race, nationality, cultural heritage, socioeconomic status, geographical area, or—and this is most likely—some combination of these and many others. Consider these examples of personal statements in which adults identify themselves with the groups that define them:

- ◆ "I am a poor African American man living in Watts."
- ◆ "I am a middle-class Asian American woman living in Los Angeles."

Individual Identity

Now consider some of the variations in interpretation that might identify, as individuals, the people who made the original statements.

- ◆ "I am a poor African American man living in Watts. I have a steady job that pays the minimum wage. I share a small apartment with two other people. I attend a church that strengthens my appreciation of my African heritage by celebrating holidays like Kwanzaa. I am a law-abiding citizen and an active member of a neighborhood protection group."

- ◆ "I am a poor African American man living in Watts. I have never held a steady job, and I depend on public assistance. I live on the streets and get an occasional meal at a mission. I have a deep-rooted resentment toward Caucasians, based on the history of my people. I do not deal drugs, but I use them when I can get them."

- ◆ "I am a middle-class Asian American woman living in Los Angeles. I am an attorney with a local law

> Most people . . . decide on the group that they belong to, or identify with, and then they decide on the qualities that make them individuals within that group.

firm. I share a large house with two other career women. I do not participate in Asian festivals since my family has been 'Americanized' for at least two generations."

◆ "I am a middle-class Asian American woman living in Los Angeles. I am a stay-at-home mother and wife. My cultural roots are still in Japan where my family lives, and I visit there several times a year. I practice the Shinto religion and make sure that my children know their heritage."

The differences in these interpretations of identity are striking. They depend on the ways in which people define the words that they use, and they are completely subjective.

Student Identity Through Family

Like adults, older students use criteria such as gender, race, nationality, cultural heritage, socioeconomic status, and geographical area to determine the groups they identify with. However, they most often see their identities through the identities of their families. Students might make statements like these: "I am the oldest boy in an African American family living in the projects in Brooklyn." "I am the youngest girl in a Mexican American family that follows the harvest and lives wherever the fruit needs to be picked." (Very young students may identify themselves simply by name. "I am Jimmy Jones" might be the statement of identity made by a child in kindergarten or first grade.)

For the most part, even older students have not yet defined the qualities that mark them as individuals within their groups. They need help with defining the words that they use, seeing diversity as a positive thing, and realizing that they can reject any negative stereotypes associated with their families' identities without rejecting their families.

Defining the Words

Many of the problems inherent in identifying with a group are caused by the ways people define the words that they use to describe things. Often the widely divergent definitions of words are influenced by the bias of the media in reporting the news. (Johnson, 1992) What does "poor" mean, for example, in the statement "I am a poor African American man living in Watts"? Obviously, it means very different things in the two statements that interpret it. The first man could have said "I am a low-income African American man living in Watts," a statement with very different overtones.

Like adults, older students use criteria such as gender, race, nationality, cultural heritage, socioeconomic status, and geographical area to determine the groups they identify with.

It is important to teach students to use words carefully, avoiding stereotypes and self-fulfilling prophesies. If people call themselves poor, they will probably act poor and unthinkingly participate in a series of actions that make them even better fit their own definition of the word.

Again, what does "Asian American" mean to the two women who use the term? Certainly not the same thing. The first woman is making a casual reference to her geographical and racial background. The second woman is identifying with her cultural and ethnic heritage. Here again, stereotypes should be avoided. (Wong, 1993)

Appreciating Diversity

Since the diversity displayed in the United States is so vast, students should be taught to look at it in the most positive way possible. Once one gets past gender and the main racial groups, the array of nationalities, cultures, socioeconomic levels, and geographical areas is overwhelming. And here too, it all depends on how people look at these various characteristics. Scholars are still arguing about what constitutes the origin and development of the American national identity. (Muller, 1994) Are Americans to be defined by their original nationalities, or are they all simply citizens of the United States? Which cultural traditions should be preserved? They would certainly be different for each person. Who should determine each person's socioeconomic class? Sociologists divide people into a multilevel arrangement of economic classes that can be quite arbitrary. Would you rather think of yourself as upper-lower class or lower-middle class? How should your geographical area be determined? Should you define yourself generally as a mid-westerner or as a Californian or more exactly as a resident of Detroit or Beverly Hills?

Students can be helped to look at all of these possibilities and choose the applicable ones that make them feel good about themselves. Self-fulfilling prophesies can, after all, work both ways.

Rejecting Negative Stereotypes

Since most people want the best for their children, they usually encourage them to break free from any negative situations. There are exceptions, of course, but in most cases families will support their children's aspirations. They might be the first ones to finish high school, the first ones to go to college, or the first ones to be financially successful.

Self-fulfilling prophesies can, after all, work both ways.

4

Students can be inspired to reach their full potentials through hearing the stories of men and women who overcame obstacles to become successful in their chosen fields. Classroom libraries should include books that tell these stories. Kathy Seal, writing in *Family Circle,* cites the work of Carol Dweck, a professor of psychology at Columbia University. In one of Dweck's studies, students chose more challenging tasks after reading books about people who succeeded because they kept trying. (Seal, 1996) Jane Goodall, the anthropologist, is a good example of this kind of person. In Goodall's 1995 article in *National Geographic,* she urges young people to take individual responsibility for the earth, for other creatures, for fellow human beings, and for themselves. (Goodall, 1995)

Let's Look at Abilities

Abilities are the second of the three components of self-image or self-concepts that will be considered here.

Multiple Intelligences

No matter what their ages, it is difficult for people to think about something until they have the words with which to form the concepts. If students are given the appropriate vocabulary for a subject, they can more readily grasp and work with the ideas. If students know that there are various kinds of intelligences, are familiar with the names of these, and understand something about the intelligences, they will be more apt to recognize these in themselves and in others.

Acquaint the students with their abilities by giving them information about the seven intelligences defined by Howard Gardner (1983, 1993) in his books *Multiple Intelligences: The Theory in Practice* and *Frames of Mind: The Theory of Multiple Intelligences.* Information about this theory is increasingly available in the popular press. In an article titled "Tap Your Child's Special Strengths" which appeared in *Family Circle's* Back-to-School Special, Ralph Blumenthal, who covers cultural news for *The New York Times*, describes Gardner's theory and gives several pages of suggestions for activities that parents could implement with their children. "The implications of this expanded view of intelligences have been sweeping," Blumenthal writes. (Blumenthal, 1996)

The Intelligences Defined

Although he reminds us that there could be many more, the seven intelligences identified by Howard Gardner in *Frames of Mind* are linguistic intelligence, logical-mathematical intelligence, spatial

Students can be inspired to reach their full potentials through hearing the stories of men and women who overcame obstacles to become successful in their chosen fields.

intelligence, musical intelligence, bodily-kinesthetic intelligence, interpersonal intelligence, and intrapersonal intelligence. (The two intelligences that are listed first are the ones we already recognize, appreciate, and teach to the most. They are the ones that assure success in school.)

Linguistic Intelligence

Linguistic intelligence is sometimes called *verbal* intelligence. It is different from the other intelligences because everyone who speaks or understands a language can be said to possess it at some level, although it is clear that some people are more linguistically talented than others. Linguistic intelligence expresses itself in words, both written and oral, and in auditory skills. People who have this kind of intelligence can learn by listening. They like to read, write, and speak, and they like to play with words. They are often seen as possessing high levels of the other intelligences simply because standard testing tools usually rely on verbal responses, no matter which type of intelligence is being assessed.

Logical-Mathematical Intelligence

Logical-mathematical intelligence includes scientific ability. It is the type of intelligence that is often called *critical thinking*. People with this kind of intelligence like to do things with data; they see patterns and relationships. They like to solve mathematical problems and play strategy games such as checkers and chess. They tend to use graphic organizers both to please themselves and to present their information to others. This kind of intelligence is highly valued in our technological society.

Spatial Intelligence

Spatial intelligence is sometimes called *visual* intelligence. People with this kind of intelligence tend to think in pictures, and they learn best from visual presentations such as movies, pictures, videos, and demonstrations with models and props. They like to draw, paint, or sculpt their ideas and often represent moods and feelings through art. They are good at reading maps and diagrams, and they enjoy solving mazes and putting together jigsaw puzzles. Spatial intelligence is often experienced and expressed through daydreaming, imagining, and pretending.

Musical Intelligence

Musical intelligence is sometimes referred to as *rhythmic* or *musical/rhythmic* intelligence. People with this kind of intelligence are sensitive to sounds, environmental as well as musical. They often sing, whistle, or hum while engaging in other activities. They love to listen to music, they may collect compact discs and tapes, and they often play instruments. People with this intelligence sing on key and can remember and vocally reproduce melodies. They may move rhythmically in time to music (or in time to an activity) or make up rhythms and songs to help them remember facts and other information. If musical intelligence is not recognized as a talent, it is often treated as a behavior problem.

Bodily-Kinesthetic Intelligence

Bodily-kinesthetic intelligence is sometimes simply called *kinesthetic* intelligence. People with this kind of intelligence process information through the sensations they feel in their bodies. They like to move around, act things out, and touch the people with whom they are talking. They are good at both small and large muscle skills and enjoy physical activities and sports of all kinds. They prefer to communicate information by demonstration or modeling. They can express emotion and mood through dance.

Interpersonal Intelligence

People with interpersonal intelligence enjoy being with friends and participating in social activities of all kinds. They are reluctant to be alone. They enjoy working in groups, learn while interacting and cooperating, and often serve as mediators in cases of disputes both in school situations and at home. Cooperative learning methods could have been designed just for them, and likewise, the designers of cooperative learning activities probably have this kind of intelligence also.

Intrapersonal Intelligence

Intrapersonal intelligence is shown through a deep awareness of inner feelings. This is the intelligence that allows people to understand themselves, their abilities, and their opinions. People with intrapersonal intelligence tend to be independent and self-directed and have strong opinions on controversial subjects. They have a great sense

Once students have internalized and are comfortable with the information about the different intelligences, they will begin to use the terminology in their ordinary speaking vocabularies.

of self-confidence and enjoy working on their own projects and just being alone.

Intelligence Clusters

Everyone who is "normal" has more than one type of intelligence. Indeed, almost everyone has several types of intelligence; some people have all of them, although some are more highly developed than others. Even interpersonal and intrapersonal intelligences can occur in the same person who learns to switch back and forth as necessity demands or the opportunity presents itself.

Let's Look at Worth or Self-Esteem

Worth or self-esteem is the third of the three components of self-image or self-concept that will be considered here.

Self-Esteem Defined

Self-esteem is one's perception of the value or worth of one's own identity and abilities. It has very little to do with the way a person is perceived from the "outside." Someone who is, from an objective point of view, extremely capable and successful may feel insignificant and insecure. Someone who is seen as incapable and unsuccessful may feel quite effective and very secure. Telling the person with a negative self-image that he or she is brilliant or wonderful has little positive impact; in fact, the result of lavish praise may be negative. (Kohn, 1993)

The Changing Picture of Self-Esteem

For many reasons, including this negative reaction to praise, an increasing number of psychologists and educators are questioning the value of trying to raise students' self-esteems either as an end in itself or as a means to improve academic performances. Thomas Moeller writes in *Education Digest* that research shows an increase in self-esteem as a result of improved academic performance rather than the other way around. (Moeller, 1994) Harold V. Stevenson echoes Moeller's ideas in *USA Today Magazine.* (Stevenson, 1996) Alfie Kohn, writing in the *Phi Delta Kappan,* is concerned about placing so much emphasis on children's psychological states rather than their learning processes. (Kohn, 1994) Other articles decrying the need to raise self-esteem abound. Among them are "I'm Terrific, You're Terrific" by Andrew Ferguson in *Washingtonian* and "Down With Self-Esteem" by Joseph Adelson in *Commentary.* (Ferguson, 1995 and Adelson, 1996)

Some psychologists and educators take a more middle-of-the-road attitude. Writing in *The New Republic,* Richard Weissbourd advis-

---

Self-esteem is one's perception of the value or worth of one's own identity and abilities.

es a balanced approach that focuses on both self-esteem and academic achievement. (Weissbourd, 1996) Others are coming to believe that self-esteem can be increased by focusing on the value of effort and persistence and on the process rather than the product. They advise "describing" instead of "judging." (Faber and Mazlish, 1995)

Optimism may also have a positive effect on self-esteem. In his recent book, *The Optimistic Child* (1995), Martin Seligman, a professor of psychology at the University of Pennsylvania, suggests several strategies to use for promoting optimism in children. These strategies include helping children to realize that setbacks are temporary, good results can be brought about through planning and effort, and hard jobs can be broken down into workable steps. He also recommends reminding children of their past successes.

One of the main themes of the new attitude toward self-esteem is the emphasis on the internal control of situations and events. People feel good about themselves if they realize that their hard work brought them success; they do not feel good about themselves if the task was too easy or they perceive that their success was a result of luck.

One of the main themes of the new attitude toward self-esteem is the emphasis on the internal control of situations and events.

Self-Esteem and Gender
Interestingly enough, and all of the research notwithstanding, the different ways that self-esteem develops—and fails to develop—in boys and girls is still a big issue. Bruce Bower writes in *Science News* that the results of a nine-year study indicate that self-esteem develops differently in boys and girls. (Bower, 1993) In *U.S. News & World Report,* Amy Saltzman writes that research shows that a girl's self-esteem declines in early adolescence, causing a corresponding decline in academic performance. Reasons for this are still being debated. (Saltzman, 1994) Victor Dwyer reports that a poll commissioned by *Maclean's* magazine indicates that teenage girls have lower self-esteems than teenage boys. (Dwyer, 1993) Coryanne Corbett, writing in *Essence,* gives tips for unlocking self-empowerment in young women, especially those of African descent. (Corbett, 1995) The interest in self-esteem may in the long run be kept alive through the women's movement.

Self-Esteem and Teenagers
In addition to the gender issue, there is the issue of age. Age groups that are seen as "at risk" are also seen as candidates for increased self-esteem. Pre-adolescents and teenagers fall into this category, and studies have been conducted on them too. Carey Goldberg reports in *The New York Times Magazine* on a study of

poor self-image in four children, ages ten through twelve. (Goldberg, 1995) In *Chatelaine,* Michael Ryval reports that studies show a connection between self-identity and self-esteem. Self-esteem can be increased in teenagers by encouraging individuality. (Ryval, 1993)

Worth or Self-Esteem in Review

Whether you believe that self-esteem is a cause or a result of academic achievement, you can still believe that it is important. It may be even more important to girls than to boys and to pre-teens and teens than to other age groups.

Self-Concept in Review

Take a look at what you have learned about self-concept by applying the components to yourself and your students.

Identity

Formulate your own personal statement as it applies to the groups with which you identify. Then expand the statement to reflect your individual identity. Help your students to complete this exercise on a level that is appropriate to their age and experience.

Ability

Analyze your own intelligences. Which ones do you recognize in yourself? Have you always had them? Are there some that you feel may lie dormant within you? What could you do about that? Encourage your students to discover and discuss their intelligences. Provide experiences that will trigger their development.

Self-Esteem

What makes you feel good about yourself? How do you react to praise? How do you react to setbacks? How do you react to success? Help your students to focus on their processes rather than their products by describing their work instead of judging it. Teach them to be optimistic by showing them how to overcome difficulties and achieve success through their own efforts.

Growing in Social Awareness

The Second Step

The development of social awareness is the second step in building a strategy for conflict resolution. Once you (and your students) can answer the question "Who am I?" it is time to pose the question "Who are you?"

The development of social awareness directs the students' attentions outward to focus on others. This is a huge jump for the kindergartner who may be just beginning to notice that there are other people in the world. Older students, who are undoubtedly already very social, often need help in directing their social skills in constructive ways. Social awareness starts with **recognition** and moves through **appreciation** to an **acknowledgment of diversity.** After people have been recognized, their individual qualities can be appreciated and their diversity can be acknowledged and enjoyed. Finally, the **adoption of a code of behavior** for dealing with others is necessary.

Social awareness starts with recognition and moves through appreciation to an acknowledgment of diversity.

11

also affect the ways in which people are perceived by others. People can certainly rise above their names, but it often takes some effort to overcome an unpleasant, or even laughable, first impression. (Bell, 1996) Names should be chosen carefully so that people will not be embarrassed by them when they are older. One author suggests that parents should give their children at least three names so that they will have a selection from which to choose. (Boyles, 1996) But, changing one's name if it is embarrassing is always an option. (Welsch, 1994) It is interesting to note that the internet has offered people the opportunity to adopt nicknames with which to identify themselves. These nicknames actually can become alternate identities with complicated social implications. (Murphy, 1994) Since students are increasingly active in the environment of computer communication, it may be both interesting and important to note the names that they adopt.

One of the most important ways in which we can show that we recognize people is to call them by name. (One of the easiest ways to offend people is to point at them and say, "Hey, you!") If everyone in a classroom knows the names of all of the other people in the classroom, you will have done away with the little exclusive groups that foment conflict. This is a simple and too often overlooked method of creating a friendly classroom. For young children, it is important because it is their only environment within a school. (Remember, a child's name may be his or her first real statement of identity.) And, for older students who move from class to class, it is crucial to have a place where one is recognized and acknowledged.

Name recognition is easily encouraged through games and activities of all kinds. It can also become part of your technique for classroom management. Students who take the roll, pass out and/or file the papers, dismiss the class, and so on, quickly become familiar with the names of their classmates and the faces that go with them.

While students are learning names, have them interview each other to discover more in-depth information. Tell them to ask for factual information such as state or country of origin, languages spoken, schools attended, number of siblings, favorite sports, and so on. These interviews can be shared orally or be bound in a class scrapbook and added to your library.

Devote one bulletin board to pictures. You can use school pictures, take pictures yourself, or ask your students to bring in snapshots. Post each student's name under his or her picture. Change the pictures occasionally. The old ones can be placed in the scrapbook with the appropriate interview forms.

Do not forget newcomers. When new students enroll in your class, remember to go through the process with them right away. Put their pictures and names up on the bulletin board. Have them interviewed by classmates and add these interviews to your class scrapbook. Give them jobs that will expose them to the names of everyone in the class.

Appreciation

When you are confident that everyone in your class is able to call everyone else by name and knows something about each person, begin to focus on positive character traits. If you model the process yourself, your students will be quick to follow. "Oh, ask Mike," you can say. "He is always willing to help." Or, "I'm sure Gina can give you the information about that assignment. She is so organized." Gradually Mike, who has had a reputation for being a troublemaker, will be seen (and will function) as the helpful one. Gina, who has been thought of as an object of pity because she is so poor, will be respected for her organizational skills. Make your statements casually, as if they should be taken for granted, but be sure to make your statements *true*. Pick a characteristic that, while often overlooked, really is there. Also, be sure to pick a characteristic that you want to have reinforced. It is probably best not to call attention to the fact that the irrepressible class clown is *funny*. Maybe he or she is also basically truthful or dependable.

Our country, which used to be thought of as a "melting pot," has become more of a "salad bowl."

Brainstorm lists of positive words with your students so that they will have the vocabulary that you want them to use. Try kind, generous, funny, happy, cheerful, nice, truthful, polite, neat, smart, good, helpful, organized, caring, busy, brave, calm, sweet, punctual, dependable, and so on. Write the words on cards and put them up in the room somewhere so that your students can use them conveniently, both orally and in writing.

Acknowledgment of Diversity

Our country, which used to be thought of as a "melting pot," has become more of a "salad bowl." People are still different and still all tossed together, but they want to keep their individual heritages alive and separate during the mixing process.

Keep your classroom wall map of the world pulled down to increase your students' awareness of the global community in which they live. Introduce and/or reinforce the concept that all

Americans are either immigrants or the descendants of immigrants. Point out to your students that everyone in the United States (in fact, on both the North and South American continents) came here from somewhere else. Even the people who are now called Native Americans came here from somewhere else. Most scientists think that they came over a land bridge from Asia when a great deal of water was frozen in glaciers, thus lowering the ocean level. (Point this area out on the map and/or globe.) Have your students find out where they, or their ancestors, came from and mark these places on the map with little flags that they can write their names on.

You can celebrate the languages that are spoken in your own classroom by having the students who are fluent in other languages teach them to interested people in the class.

The Conference on College Composition and Communication (CCCC) recognizes multiculturalism in education with its "students' right to their own language" policy. (Smitherman, 1995) You can celebrate the languages that are spoken in your own classroom by having the students who are fluent in other languages teach them to interested people in the class. Set aside fifteen minutes every day and have the students divide into groups with a student "teacher" for short language classes. Learn some words and phrases yourself. Greet your class each morning in a different language. (A chart of greetings is on page 15.)

You can, of course, celebrate diversity in many, many ways. Consider inviting parents to share their cultural heritages in your classroom, especially around the time of important holidays and festivals. Or, have a multicultural fair, featuring ethnic foods and traditions. Bring your daily newspaper to school and encourage your students to keep informed about what is going on around the world. Invite the students to read and share books about other countries and other customs. If your classroom is a microcosm of diversity, your students will appreciate your sensitivity. If your classroom does not have a diverse population, your students will probably benefit from this positive exposure to the real world.

[If your school district has adopted a full inclusion policy, you may be handling a different kind of diversity. Students with extreme differences in abilities in the regular classroom present a new challenge to teachers and students alike. If you are not experienced in or trained for this educational innovation, be sure to avail yourself of any help offered by your school district and all of the support you can get from the special education teachers. This is still a controversial program. An article titled "Should School Systems Move Toward Full Inclusion?" in *CQ Researcher* (1993) describes both sides of the debate. However, many extremely partisan articles can be found on both sides of the question. A column

Hello Chart

Language	Greeting	Pronunciation
English	Hello	(hel-LO)
Spanish	Hola	(OH-la)
Hawaiian	Aloha	(ah-LO-ha)
Swahili	Jambo	(JAHM-bo)
French	Bonjour	(bon-zhoor)
Arabic	Salaam	(sah-LAHM)
Japanese	Konnichiwa	(kon-nichi-WAH)
Hindi	Namaste	(nam-ahs-TAY)
German	Guten tag	(GU-ten TAHG)
Yiddish	Shalom	(sha-LOHM)
Russian	Priviet	(preev-YET)

in the *Phi Delta Kappan*, "W(h)ither Full Inclusion?" describes the difficulties (1995), and Thomas Murphy, writing in the *National Review* (1994), condemns the whole program.]

Adoption of a Code of Behavior

Finally, an acceptable code of behavior for dealing with others can be adopted and practiced. This is really just another way of saying that we should all, adults and children alike, learn and use good manners. Many students, especially pre-adolescents and adolescents, go through a stage when they think that manners are not "cool." It is important to address this attitude because the use of simple good manners is a major element in avoiding conflict. Rudeness, on the other hand, is a major cause of conflict.

U.S. News & World Report has acknowledged the importance of this problem by featuring it as a cover story which it called "The American Uncivil Wars: How Crude, Rude and Obnoxious Behavior Has Replaced Good Manners and Why That Hurts Our Politics and Power." In the related article, John Marks reports that poll results indicate that 90% of Americans believe that incivility in the United States is a serious problem. Many people believe that rude behavior contributes to violence and that efforts should be made to reverse this social trend. (Marks, 1996) *Los Angeles Magazine* joined the trend with "Poise'n the Hood: There's Nothing Wrong With America a Little Etiquette Couldn't Cure." This article by Jeff MacGregor promotes the idea of charm schools or tutoring to help people build their social skills with the objective of reducing the incidence of violence. (MacGregor, 1996)

Magazines for parents have also addressed this problem. In *Parenting*, Joyce Maynard equates having good manners with showing respect and consideration for others. (Maynard, 1995) Patricia McCormick, writing in *Parents Magazine*, agrees and also adds that children can be taught that good manners make them more enjoyable to be with. (McCormick, 1994)

William Kreidler, writing in *Instructor*, brings teachers into the picture with an article titled "Cultivating Courtesy: How to Turn Rude Dudes Into Courtesy Kids." He describes a number of classroom activities for building courtesy, but his main thrust is that in order to be successful, teachers must be models of courteous behavior. (Kreidler, 1995)

There are five major areas in which students should learn to use appropriate manners: in the home, in the classroom, in the school,

Many students, especially pre-adolescents and adolescents go through a stage when they think that manners are not "cool."

in any place where they might be seen as representatives of their school, and in the world at large where they cannot help but be seen as representatives of youth as a group or class.

It is popular today to "demonize" young people, teenagers in particular. They are often depicted in the media as vicious and hardened criminals and in the justice system as mature adults. As a corollary of this, however, any young person who is seen doing anything good—brave, helpful, or just polite—will most likely inspire a letter to the editor of the local paper. For this reason, it seems possible that students who have learned just basic good manners could help to turn the tide of public opinion in favor of youth. Even if the effort falls short of that mark, basic good manners will reduce the daily incidence of conflict situations in the classroom and the school.

Do whatever you have to do to convince your students that manners are an important part of life. To the purist who objects, using the argument that manners are just on the surface, you can reply that that is just where they belong. They are supposed to provide a cushion, or buffer zone, between people to keep the sharp edges from rubbing together and creating sparks.

Very young children can be provided with a few "magic words" that will get them through most situations: please, thank you, you're welcome, excuse me, may I, and so on. If teachers, as well as the other adults with whom children come into contact, consistently model the use of these words, you will not have to do much else. Unfortunately, however, many adults, including teachers, are not polite to young people. They issue abrupt commands, and they correct behavior by using insulting language and demeaning remarks. If your students are exposed to adults of this type, you will have a much bigger job ahead of you.

Older students should be using the same words, although you would probably be well-advised to call them "basic words" or "key words." Start the campaign for basic politeness on a classroom level by giving out meaningful rewards—homework passes, free time awards, coupons good for free cookies in the school cafeteria—for courteous behavior that you observe. If students begin to be flamboyantly polite in order to collect rewards, consider that to be all the better. The more often and the more publicly people are polite, the easier it becomes.

Social Awareness in Review
Take a look at what you have learned about social awareness by applying the components to yourself and your students.

> **Do whatever you have to do to convince your students that manners are an important part of life.**

17

Recognition

How are you doing with your program of having everybody know everybody else's names? Are the pictures and names on the bulletin board current? What about that new student? Have you asked someone to run him through the process of learning names and matching them with faces?

Appreciation

Can you associate each person in your class with at least one positive quality? Have your positive comments had an effect on the way people in your class perceive one another?

Acknowledgment of Diversity

Is the classroom map still pulled down? What languages have been introduced? Have you celebrated any ethnic holidays? If you have a full-inclusion classroom, have you worked on ways to help your students accept one another?

Adoption of a Code of Behavior

Have you run a quality check on your own manners with students? Do you always model the manners that you want them to use? Have you helped your students to make the connection between having good manners and reversing the incidence of violence?

Acquiring Communication Skills

Another Important Step

Acquiring communication skills is another important step in building a foundation for the development of a strategy for conflict resolution. Once you (and your students) can answer the questions "Who am I?" and "Who are you?" it is time to pose the question "Can we talk?"

True communication consists of three parts—a message is sent, it is received, and there is some kind of response. This can be shown graphically as a circular process, since the response leads to another message or, in fact, becomes the next message. People can express themselves as much as they want, but if there is no one to receive the message and respond to it, they have not truly communicated.

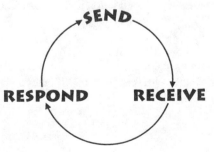

Reasons for Communication

In general, people communicate in order to share facts, opinions, and emotions or feelings. The messages connected with conflict situations usually communicate emotions. Even if they are basically made up of facts and opinions, they are charged with emotions because of the conflict or the danger of conflict. In an article in *Instructor* entitled "Tell It Like It Is: How to Ward Off Conflicts by Improving Kids' Communication Skills," William Kreidler writes that according to a recent survey, miscommunication is the cause of 85% of conflicts between school children. Improving their communication skills is the surest way to correct this situation. (Kreidler, 1996)

The Ability to Communicate

The messages
connected with conflict
situations usually
communicate emotions.

Students have as much a right as anyone else to say how they feel and what they want. It is important, however, especially in cases about which they feel strongly, that they have information about and practice in sending a clear message, receiving the message that was sent, and making an appropriate response. Students usually get more practice in listening than in speaking because teachers emphasize listening skills in the classroom. Although listening is of vital importance in the oral communication process, it can never be more important than the message that is sent or the response that is made. Both of these components of the communication process require the ability to use spoken language. Becoming proficient in this ability requires both instruction and a great deal of practice.

June Bowser, writing in the *English Journal,* emphasizes that students should be encouraged to talk spontaneously on topics that interest them. She suggests interviewing people as an activity that will encourage talking. (Bowser, 1993) Joseph Tsujimoto, writing in the same publication, reminds teachers that speaking (or talking) is a learning tool and is as important to classroom learning as are writing, reading, and listening. He feels that students should be given the opportunity to articulate what they think or feel about anything and that it is important for teachers to create an environment in which students feel secure enough to talk. (Tsujimoto, 1993)

Sending the Message

The act of sending a clear message will be more effective if students learn to express themselves in "I" messages rather than "You" messages.

"You" messages are words that attack and blame. Here are two "You" messages:

- You always interrupt me and make me forget what I want to say!
- You never ask before you borrow something of mine!

"I" messages express the feelings of the person who is speaking. Here are the same two situations expressed in "I" messages:

- I feel frustrated when you interrupt me, and it makes me forget what I want to say. I want to finish what I'm saying without being interrupted.
- I feel angry when you borrow something of mine without asking. I want to be asked first so that I can decide.

To make "I" messages easier for your students, give them a formula like this one. Post the skeleton formula in the classroom for easy reference:

I feel _____ when _____

_____.

I want _____.

Be prepared to seize the moment in your classroom and have the students rephrase their actual "You" messages into "I" messages right away.

Have your students practice turning "You" messages into "I" messages. Use the samples to make up some relevant messages of your own. Also, be prepared to seize the moment in your classroom and have the students rephrase their actual "You" messages into "I" messages right away. It takes a lot of practice to overcome what is probably a well-rehearsed habit. Listen for students who are attacking one another with "You" messages and ask them to translate, using the formula given above.

If you hear a student say a "You" message:

- You always mess up my stuff. Why don't you look where you're going!

ask the student for an "I" message:

- I feel angry when my stuff gets messed up. I want you to look where you are going.

Be sure to remind your students that the more words they know, the more clearly they can communicate their feelings. They can make their "I" messages reflect and express their feelings more accurately by polishing and refining their uses of feeling words. Have your students use a dictionary and/or thesaurus to find synonyms for commonly used words such as angry, sad, happy, surprised, and disappointed. Post the lists around the classroom so that they can be used.

Make sure that you model "I" messages constantly. It is not fair to say "This class is always noisy! You embarrass me in front of the other teachers." Rephrase your statements into "I" messages.

```
I feel _____ when _____

_____.

I want _____.
```

Receiving the Message

"I" messages are just the first part of the communication process. In order to make sure the message that is received is the same as the message that was sent, students should learn a technique known as active listening. In this technique, the message is mirrored back to the sender/speaker by the receiver/listener.

This kind of listening always seems artificial and stilted at first, but with use it becomes more natural. And unless people learn how to do it, "I" messages, no matter how clear, will not be effective. Encouraging this kind of listening is largely dependent upon teacher behavior. Writing in *Childhood Education,* Mary Jalongo stresses the idea that teachers should model the technique and encourage its use among students. (Jalongo, 1995)

The first step in active listening is repeating what was said. So an easy way to teach active listening is simply to reverse the formula for an "I" message:

```
You feel _____ when_____

_____.

You want _____.
```

You can then add the second step, which is rephrasing the information to show that it was understood. Tell your students that, in real life, active listeners usually move past just repeating what they hear to restating it in their own words. This seems more natural, and it also shows whether or not the listener really understands what was said.

"I" Message: I hate it when you tease me about my freckles. I want you to stop.

Active Listening: You hate it when I tease you about your freckles. You want me to stop.

Message Restated: You want me to stop teasing you about your freckles because you hate it.

Many students will think that this whole process is hysterically funny or an insult to their intelligence. However, it is an exercise that is vital to communication and, in combination with the ability to send clear "I" messages, forms the basis for assertiveness which is one of the tools for conflict resolution to be considered later. You can assure skeptical students of the fact that many adults have paid for seminars where they were taught how to do what the students are learning.

You can provide practice in these techniques by writing a number of "You" statements and having the students work in small groups to restate messages first as "I" messages, then in the active listening formula, and then restated to show understanding. When everyone has completed the task, get together in a large group, read the restatements aloud, and discuss the results. You can also have the students role-play some situations using both formula and non-formula active listening responses to "I" messages.

Responding to the Message

After a clear message has been sent and accurately received, there are several ways of responding to the message. The restatement of the message to show understanding is the first response. Agreement, an apology, or a promise to change the behavior that elicited the original message might be the second response. However, there is still another response to communications that are sent in "I" messages and received through active listening. It is the response that gives information about how the situation looks from the other person's perspective. The following is an example.

1st person/"I" Message: I was disappointed when you didn't call me with the homework assignment. I would like you to be more dependable.

You can assure skeptical students of the fact that many adults have paid for seminars where they were taught how to do what the students are learning.

2nd person/Active Listening: I can hear that you feel like I let you down about the homework assignment. You were depending on me but . . . . *Can I tell you what happened?*

"Can I tell you what happened?" introduces the second person's perspective. At this point the second person gives an "I" message, and the whole process starts again.

Communicating Emotions in Review

Take a look at what you have learned about communicating emotions by applying the components to yourself and your students.

Sending "I" Messages

Are you able to formulate a clear "I" message that tells how you feel and what you want? Do you have a vocabulary of feeling words that helps express your feelings?

Listening Actively

Can you use the active listening formula to restate the "I" message you heard? Can you restate what you heard to show understanding?

Responding Appropriately

Can you respond by rephrasing the message? Can you express agreement, give an apology, or agree to change the original behavior if these responses are appropriate? Finally, can you give information from your own perspective with another "I" message? Depending on the circumstances, you need to be able to do all of these things in order to communicate effectively.

Reinforcing the Skills

After your students have had an opportunity to practice and perfect their skills in communicating emotions, let them pass on their knowledge to other students. Invite another class to be the "students" and encourage the members of your class to plan some demonstrations and some teaching strategies to pass on what they have learned.

You can have your class teach in partners with their "students" or have small groups teach small groups. Either way, have everyone meet in a large group at the end of each lesson to demonstrate what they have learned.

Besides giving others the benefits of their information, the members of your class will internalize what they have learned on a deeper level as they explain the various skills involved in the oral communication of feelings. They will also be practicing their oral communication skills just through the process of teaching them to others.

After your students have had an opportunity to practice and perfect their skills in communicating emotions, let them pass on their knowledge to other students.

Another Communication Style

There is more than one kind of oral message and more than one listening style, but the skills are transferable; skill in one area of communication enhances skill in the others. Sometimes people talk about facts and opinions rather than feelings, and sometimes we are not able to listen actively in the sense of repeating aloud what we hear. Nevertheless, the person sending the message must state it clearly, the person receiving the message must understand it, and there must be some response or feedback to make the communication process work.

When the sender/speaker is talking about facts and opinions, these need to be organized and delivered in such a way that the receiver/listener can take them in. The receiver/listener, who can also be called the audience, has the responsibility of trying to understand what is being said. This comprehension must then be communicated back to the speaker. How can this be done?

Have your students prepare short talks on any subjects that interest them. This will be most effective if they talk about something that is important to them, something that they want the other people in the class to know about too. In giving their talks to the class, they will be "sending" (orally communicating) facts and opinions rather than feelings.

Have your students discuss their responsibilities as speakers—they should try to make their talks clear and organized, speak in voices that can be heard, and try to establish eye contact with members of their audience.

Have your students discuss their responsibilities as listeners—they should be quiet and attentive, have positive attitudes toward the speaker and the information, and try to take in the information. They should be silent active listeners, repeating the information to themselves inside their heads.

Before beginning the presentation of the speeches, discuss audience responses. The two main audience responses (excluding the clapping at the end of the speech) are eye contact and body language.

There is more than one kind of oral message and more than one listening style, but the skills are transferable; skill in one area of communication enhances skill in the others.

Eye Contact: This is as much a part of responding as it is of sending. The speaker who is trying to establish eye contact does not have a chance if everyone in the audience is looking at the ceiling or out the window.

Body Language: This response is really important. It lets the speaker know that the audience is interested. Appropriate body language while listening and responding to a speaker can include both posture and gestures. An audience member who leans forward slightly (posture) and nods his or her head (gesture) at important points is giving a positive response.

Have the students brainstorm some possible negative responses. (Leaning back, looking around or at the ceiling, yawning, and staring blankly straight ahead are a few likely examples.)

A question-and-answer period at the end of a speech is another possible audience response. If you would like to include this response, the speaker should be warned ahead of time that he or she will be expected to answer questions. Answering questions about the material will probably require more in-depth preparation. The audience should be prepared for this activity too. Each question should be phrased politely and be a request for more information about something of interest to the person asking the question. Positive comments about the material and/or presentation are a possibility also. Caution the audience/responders about the inappropriateness of making negative comments.

Set aside time for the presentation of the speeches. After all of the speeches have been presented, have each student fill out two checklists (sample checklists are on page 28), one from the speaker's point of view and the other from the audience member's point of view.

Compare and discuss the whole experience as well as the results of the checklists. You can use the questions on page 27 to guide your discussion. In addition, encourage your students to express their feelings by using "I" messages, thus blending the two communication styles. Remind them of the formula for these messages. For example:

I feel good about my speech because my information was interesting.

I'd like to have more practice in organizing my ideas.

A question-and-answer period at the end of a speech is another possible audience response.

Another Communication Style in Review

Take a look at what you have learned about communicating facts and opinions by applying the components to yourself and your students.

The Sender/Speaker

What responsibilities did you have as the sender/speaker? Was your information interesting? Were your ideas clear and organized? Did you speak in a voice that could be heard? Did you pronounce your words clearly? Did you try to establish eye contact with each member of the audience whether it consisted of a group of people or just one person? If there was a question-and-answer period after your presentation, were you prepared to give more information? Did you know how to respond to positive comments? What part of your presentation would you improve upon if you were to do it again?

The Receiver/Listener/Audience

What responsibilities did you have as the receiver/listener/audience? Were you quiet and attentive? Did you have a positive attitude toward the speaker and the information and try to take in what was being said? Have you tried being a silent active listener by repeating the information to yourself inside your head? If you were to do it again, is there anything you would improve upon or do differently?

The Receiver/Responder/Audience

What responsibilities did you have as the receiver/responder/audience? Did you respond to the speaker with positive body language? What postures or gestures did you try? What postures or gestures did you consciously avoid? If there was a question-and-answer period after the presentation, did you try to formulate good questions? Were you able to make positive comments? If you were to do it again, is there anything you would improve upon or do differently?

Speech Checklists

Name _____ Date _____

Directions: Analyze your participation in this speech activity. Check off the boxes which pertain to your experience.

When I Was the Speaker

I felt as if the audience heard me because . . .

❑ . . . no one talked.

❑ . . . they looked interested.

❑ . . . they looked at me.

❑ . . . I was able to make eye contact.

❑ . . . they nodded at the important points.

When I Was the Audience

I responded by . . .

❑ . . . paying attention.

❑ . . . looking interested.

❑ . . . looking at the speaker.

❑ . . . making eye contact.

❑ . . . nodding at important points.

Developing Respect and Empathy

Why Should I Care?

Respect and empathy (which has been called the most uncomfortable of human emotions) are intense feelings for anyone, especially children and young people, but they are basic to our humanity. Now that we have answered the following questions:

- ◆ "Who am I?"
- ◆ "Who are you?"
- ◆ "Can we talk?"

it is time to ask the question "Why should I care?" The answer to this question is "I care because I know what you mean and I know how you feel." According to Dorothy Rich in *MegaSkills,* caring connects people and establishes a sense of community. "It's about consideration, about being interested in others, about listening to and learning from them." (Rich, 1992)

The Words Themselves

Make sure that your students know and can apply the meanings of the words that both you and they will be using. What exactly is *respect*? What is *disrespect*? What is *sympathy*? What is *empathy*? What makes sympathy and empathy different from each other? Have your students look up the words and read the definitions aloud as a basis for a class discussion. Give your own examples and have them share theirs. Have they experienced empathy? When? Why? What were the circumstances?

> Respect and empathy are intense feelings for anyone, especially children and young people, but they are basic to our humanity.

What Resources Do I Have?

The school experience is fairly insulated from the events of real life. Conflict and even violence certainly manage to thrust their way in, but we see and hear very little about the routine heroism shown by ordinary people in their daily lives. We gather young people from every conceivable environment, put them together in small rooms and, at least in many cases, try to teach them all of the same things at the same time. In this situation, what resources do we have for helping them to develop respect and empathy for each other and for other people? There are probably two main resources in every classroom for us to draw from—the students themselves and the events of life as they are depicted in literature.

Students as a Resource

If your students have come to know themselves and one another and have learned to communicate among themselves, they may have some interesting and important stories to tell. If your classroom is a place where trust has grown, they may want to share their stories there. If you are brave enough, you may let them. Some students may have experienced the horrors of war before arriving in this country. Other students may have experienced horrors right here. Some students will be grieving because of a death or a divorce. Others may be running a household or taking care of a sick parent or grandparent. Remember, you will undoubtedly hear more than you ever wanted to know. However, before you ever allow this to happen, you must grapple with the concept of confidentiality.

Confidentiality in the Classroom

Students must be assured of absolute confidentiality concerning anything they say in your (their) classroom. Because of this, you will have to make at least one unbreakable rule before you start. If anyone tells a story indicating that a law has been broken, you will have to report it. Some students may tell their stories for just that reason, because they are sure that you will know who to tell and what to do. However, others will be warned not to incriminate themselves or the people they care about. Other than that one exception, anything that is said in your classroom stays in the classroom, unless someone asks you for help. You may want to arm yourself with knowledge of the helping agencies in your community, just in case.

It will probably take a lot of talking on your part to explain the responsibility of keeping everything confidential, but no student should share his or her personal history until everyone understands and promises to abide by the concept. Obviously, most of

> There are probably two main resources in every classroom for us to draw from—the students themselves and the events of life as they are depicted in literature.

your classroom business will be ordinary and routine. For this reasons, you should have a signal, a code word, or a special place for students to share information that they want to keep confidential. You might meet in a circle with younger students or call a classroom meeting with older ones, always with the reminder that whatever information is shared needs to be kept confidential.

The Benefits to Be Gained

Some of the information shared by your students will probably be in the form of complaints about situations in which they find themselves. This kind of sharing is perfectly legitimate and allows them to vent and blow off steam. It also gives other students a chance to identify and to nod in agreement and support. Some students may want to offer a word of advice or encouragement.

Some of the information shared by your students will be more dramatic, stories of things that they have experienced or are experiencing. The shy, quiet boy who avoids active participation in sports may tell the saga of his family's escape by boat from a country at war. The girl who seems happy and well-adjusted but who tries to avoid making friends may talk about the family members she had to leave behind in order to come to the United States. The girl who seems too tired to take part in class discussions may tell about the beloved grandmother she cares for in the evenings while her mother is at work. The boy who never has his homework done on time may talk about his after-school job which supports his family. Many students may describe the problems encountered in moving from one language and set of customs at home to another language and set of customs at school.

All of the information shared by your students will help you to increase their respect and empathy for one another and, by extension, for other people in the world. It will also give you information that you can use for matching up study partners and forming cooperative groups with members who will enjoy or will benefit from working together.

Literature as a Resource

While your students are developing the kind of trust and commitment to confidentiality that will be required for sharing their experiences, you can tap into literature as a resource for teaching respect and empathy along with positive conflict resolution skills. (Luke and Myers, 1994) The stories you choose may also trigger the sharing of personal experiences by your students. Just choose your topic.

All of the information shared by your students will help you to increase their respect and empathy for one another and, by extension, for other people in the world.

The lists of topics and books that follow are not intended to be complete or comprehensive; they are simply samples and suggestions. Most of the topics can easily be related to your social studies curriculum and will add the in-depth dimension of personalized experiences to the periods you are studying. You can use topics of your own too, of course.

After you have chosen a topic and selected the books to go with it, make up sets of questions to stimulate discussions. Questions for each book can be divided into two categories:

◆ "I Know What You Mean" should consist of questions based on the facts in the book and the inferences that can be drawn from them.

◆ "I Know How You Feel" should consist of questions about the feelings described in the book and/or the feelings that the story may elicit from the reader.

A set of sample questions is included for the first book.

(The suggested books range across the grade levels. They are coded for your convenience: P stands for primary, I for intermediate, and C for challenging. NF indicates non-fiction. Many of the books written for younger students are also excellent quick read-aloud books for older students because they introduce complicated concepts with a minimum of words and help to facilitate discussions. Take advantage of these excellent books to "hook" student attention and encourage your students to further explore the subjects on their own.)

Immigration

Give your students information about the problems faced by immigrants in the countries that they came from, on their journeys, and in their new country, the United States.

Molly's Pilgrim by Barbara Cohen (Lothrop, Lee & Shepard Books, 1983)—P

This is the story of a turn-of-the-century Russian Jewish immigrant going to school in the United States.

◆ I Know What You Mean:

Why did Molly's family come to the United States? (They were escaping religious persecution.) How did they get here? (Since they came from Russia, they probably came in a large

> **After you have chosen a topic and selected the books to go with it, make up sets of questions to stimulate discussions.**

ship, perhaps in steerage class. Ask someone to look up "steerage" and read the definition to the class. The immigrants probably would have been crowded into dark, smelly areas. They would have slept in narrow bunk beds. Their trip would have taken place sometime in the late 1800s to the early 1900s when Jews were the targets of religious persecution in Russia. Ask someone to look up the word "persecution" and read the definition to the class.) Why did they leave New York City? (They left to escape poor working and living conditions.) Why did Molly stop telling her mama about what went on in school? (She wanted to keep her mother from going to school and talking to the teacher.)

◆ I Know How You Feel:

Why did some of the students make fun of Molly? Why did some people think that it was bad to be different? Has anyone ever made fun of you because of your religion or the way you look or talk? How did you feel? What did you do or say? Has this ever happened to someone you know?

Ellis Island: New Hope in a New Land by William Jay Jacobs (Macmillan Child Group, 1990)—NF

This is an interesting account of the role Ellis Island played in the history of American immigration. It includes information about the fears people experienced as they waited to see if they would pass the physical and psychological examinations that would either allow them to land in New York or condemn them to go back to where they came from.

Journey to America by Sonia Levitin (Macmillan, 1986)—C

This book portrays the hardships experienced by Jewish families trying to escape Hitler's Germany in the days preceding World War II.

Lupita Mañana by Patricia Beatty (Beech Tree Books, 1992)—C

The main characters in this book are a brother and sister from Mexico who cross the border in search of jobs in the United States. They end up working in the fields.

Different Is Okay
Give your students the opportunity to think about differences as interesting rather than threatening.

Oliver Button Is a Sissy by Tomie dePaola (Harcourt Brace Jovanovich, Inc., 1979)—P

Oliver Button's interests are different from those of the other boys and the kids call him a sissy, especially when his mother and father enroll him in dancing school for the exercise.

Mrs. Katz and Tush by Patricia Polaco (Bantam, 1992)—P

This heartwarming story emphasizes that neither race, religion, nor age differences need be barriers to friendship and understanding.

The Hundred Dresses by Eleanor Estes (Harcourt Brace Jovanovich, Inc., 1974)—I

This is a story of a young girl who is the object of teasing in school. It describes the effects of prejudice on both the victim and the victimizer.

Berries Goodman by Emily Cheney Neville (Harper Collins, 1965)—I

The main character's life becomes complicated when his family moves from New York City to the suburbs and he discovers the existence of religious prejudice in his new neighborhood.

The Pinballs by Betsy Byars (Harper & Row, 1977)—I

Three boys living in a foster home become friends and learn to pull together and make the choices that will help them gain control of their lives.

Next-Door Neighbors by Sarah Ellis (Dell, 1992)—I

Friendship between children and a Chinese man who is employed as a gardener and cook is prevented because of racial and socioeconomic prejudice.

The Summer of the Swans by Betsy Byars (Puffin, 1981)—C

Sara spends the summer feeling miserable about herself until an experience with her younger brother, who is mentally handicapped, helps her to get her priorities in order.

Cultural Heritage
Give your students insight (through literature) to the attachment of immigrants to their cultural heritages. Talk about the mixed feelings that people might have about loyalty to their original countries and to their new ones.

Hello, My Name Is Scrambled Eggs by Jamie Gilson (Simon & Schuster, 1986)—I

A well-meaning seventh grader tries to Americanize a newly arrived Vietnamese immigrant with hilarious results. This leads to a sensitive understanding of the problems faced by immigrants.

The Land I Lost: Adventures of a Boy in Vietnam by Huynh Quang Nhuong (HarpC Child Bks., 1982)—NF

This is a collection of autobiographical sketches in which the author shares his memories of growing up in Vietnam. It is a beautiful book that has won many awards, and it includes an introspective introduction by the author who now lives in the United States.

We Adopted You, Benjamin Koo by Linda Walvoord Girard (Albert Whitman, 1989)—I

This book depicts the particular challenges faced by students involved in multicultural adoptions.

Lion Dancer: Ernie Wan's Chinese New Year by Kate Waters and Madeline Slovenz-Low (Scholastic, 1990)—NF

This book, set in New York City's Chinatown, describes the traditions of the Chinese New Year as they are preserved and celebrated in the United States by a Chinese-American family.

Death and Remembrance
Give your students the opportunity to experience (within the safety of literature) respect and empathy for someone who is dying or someone who is grieving.

Everett Anderson's Good-bye by Lucy Clifton (Henry Holt, 1983)—P

After the death of his father, a little boy moves through the five classic stages of grief. Young readers (or listeners) who have lost a loved one will find comfort in this book.

The Tenth Good Thing About Barney by Judith Viorst (Aladdin, 1988)—P

Anyone who has ever experienced the loss of a pet will identify with this story as a boy mourns the death of his cat and makes a list of good things to say about him at his funeral.

Sadako and the Thousand Paper Cranes by Eleanor Coerr (Dell, 1979)—I

Sadako, who lives in Hiroshima, discovers that she has leukemia caused by radiation from the atom bomb. This book is based on a true story, and the young girl who lived and died in Hiroshima, and is remembered in the story, is honored each year on Peace Day.

Annie and the Old One by Miska Miles (Little Brown, 1971)—I

Annie's happy Navaho world is spoiled when her cherished grandmother, the Old One, announces that she will die when the rug she is weaving is finished and taken down from the loom.

Bridge to Terabithia by Katherine Paterson (Harper, 1987)—C
A boy and girl become best friends and create a magical kingdom together. The girl dies and the boy struggles with, and finally resolves, his grief.

Tuck Everlasting by Natalie Babbitt (Farrar, Straus, and Giroux, 1985)—C

A young girl who discovers the Tuck family's secret of everlasting life must decide whether or not she wants to join them.

Respect and Empathy in Review
Take a look at what you have learned about respect and empathy by applying these components of caring to yourself and your students.

Students as a Resource
Do your students feel that their classroom is a safe and supportive environment in which they may share their experiences and feelings? Do they understand and respect the idea of confidentiality? Have you provided yourself with a list of community resources in case anyone needs help?

Literature as a Resource
Have you tried using literature as a resource by sharing stories that engender feelings of respect and empathy in your students? Which topics do they respond to the most?

Making Appropriate Choices

Age-Appropriate Concerns

The basic ideas connected with the first four topics in this book—self-concepts, social awareness, communication skills, and respect and empathy—extend across all of the grade levels, starting with the smallest children. Then, somewhere between third and fifth grade, something else should be added to the mix. Many students begin to feel strongly about the necessity for **rules**, the importance of **fairness** and **justice**, and the value of **competition**. Although these are certainly excellent standards, they can—if rigidly adhered to and carried to extremes—escalate conflict situations rather than resolve them. These standards must be balanced by the awareness of other possibilities such as **self-direction**, compassion, consideration of **extenuating circumstances**, and **cooperation**. Rules must sometimes be broken; justice must be tempered with mercy; fairness can be modified for some exceptions; and competition should often be replaced with teamwork.

Rules and Self-Direction

Although we certainly want students to be able to recognize and follow rules, we also want them to be able to use intelligent self-direction in cases where the rules are unfair, unnecessary, or morally wrong. One has only to think of the Holocaust in Nazi

Although we certainly want students to be able to recognize and follow rules, we also want them to be able to use intelligent self-direction in cases where the rules are unfair, unnecessary, or morally wrong.

37

Germany for an example of how people can be persuaded to follow rules that are insanely immoral. There are, of course, other situations that do not involve ethical choices but are merely preferences. Many famous people—scientists, artists, explorers, performers, and so on—have rejected the ordinary "rules" or the accepted standards of their professions to follow their own paths to greatness.

Students should be encouraged to evaluate rules, think about which ones apply to them and in which circumstances, and decide whether they prefer to follow rules or exercise self-direction. It is harder, of course, to exercise self-direction, and very often the self-directed person (after agonizing over the decision) will choose the same course as the person who is blindly following the rules. Ask your students to consider some everyday rules such as traffic regulations. They all know that it is against the law to jay-walk. What would they do if going to the nearest corner to cross the street would be out of their way? What would they do if they saw a small child wander into the street in the middle of the block? Also, consider school rules. Undoubtedly, your school has a rule about running in the halls. What would your students decide to do if they were late to class? What if someone was seriously hurt on the playground and the nearest phone was in the school office? Consider a situation that is not an emergency and in which they would have more time to think. Certainly all of the students have taken important standardized tests before which they were warned about the consequences of talking or leaving their seats. What would they do if they wanted to tell a friend something? What if they noticed that smoke was coming from the roof of a building across the street from the school?

The examples given deal with matters of little personal consequences, but they will alert the students to the possibility of deciding when the rules apply and when they can be ignored. In order to consider more important issues, discuss some famous people in the news or from your current social studies text. Ask your students if they think that those people were following the rules or if they were self-directed. Ask them to justify their opinions with examples.

As a final activity, give your students the opportunity to think about whether they prefer to follow rules that have been made for them or to exercise self-direction, and then ask them to apply this insight to career planning. Discuss a variety of careers. Which ones require people to follow sets of strict rules? Which ones reward people who are self-directed? In light of what they have

Students should be encouraged to evaluate rules, think about which ones apply to them and in which circumstances, and decide whether they prefer to follow rules or exercise self-direction.

discovered about their own reactions to following rules, are there some careers that they should think about? Are there some careers that they should avoid? If a self-directed person has a great desire to follow a career with many rules, would he or she be able to adjust? Could a person who is comfortable with rules be happy in a career that requires self-direction?

Fairness and Extenuating Circumstances

Although most people pay lip service to the idea of equal treatment, they are usually quite ready to make exceptions. Give your students the opportunity to compare the idea of equal treatment (fairness) with the reality of special (extenuating) circumstances. Make sure that you are all using the related vocabulary the same way before you start your discussion. You can have the students look up *fair, equal, extenuating, special, exception,* and any other words that you think are necessary, and read the definitions to the class.

Students from about third grade and above like everything to be fair.

Students from about third grade and above like everything to be fair. However, as we all must learn, life is not always fair. Discuss the situations described below. Then ask your students to think of other circumstances that might require special, rather than equal, treatment.

- ◆ There will be a physical fitness test today that you must pass. Your left arm will be in a cast until next month and chin-ups are an important part of the test. Do you think you should get special treatment?

- ◆ You dropped a contact lens on the bus coming to school and someone stepped on it. Should you get bad grades because you won't be able to read words and numbers?

- ◆ In order for the game to be really fair, the same rules should apply to everyone. One boy is in a wheelchair and another is on crutches. Neither can run. Will you still let them play?

These are all situations based on physical limitations, but there are others that involve religious choices.

- ◆ There are rules about uniforms in your soccer league but one girl always covers her head with a shawl because of her religious beliefs. Should she be allowed to play? What will you do if the other team objects? (A case like this was reported in the news. After many league games, the coach of one team objected to the head covering. Rather than put their player in a difficult ethical position, the team forfeited the game.)

◆ Your class is going on a field trip to a museum and some of the mothers have volunteered to provide a hot dog lunch in a nearby park for a midday break. Some of the students do not eat pork. Some do not eat meat at all. Should special food be provided for them, or should they fill up on salad, potato chips, and dessert?

All of these situations could be decided either way. There are no rigid rules about fairness and extenuating circumstances. The outcomes always depend upon the values held by the person or people making the decisions. As students discuss each case, ask them why they made their decisions.

You will be aware, of course, that this can be a delicate topic if there are students in your class who are sensitive about having some special circumstances of their own. You may want to skip this topic altogether, give it just a touch, or use the opportunity to shed some light on a dark area.

Justice and Compassion

The idea of tempering justice with compassion is almost parallel to the idea of modifying fairness because of special circumstances, but not quite. Special and extenuating circumstances actually exist; they are there to be considered and evaluated. Compassion, on the other hand, is an emotional reaction. Webster's defines compassion as "sorrow for the suffering or trouble of another . . . accompanied by an urge to help." (Webster's, 1994) No extenuating or special circumstances have to exist.

Have your students define and compare justice and compassion. Is it always necessary or wise to be compassionate? Are justice and compassion common concerns? Our system of laws and courts is called the "justice system." Why don't we have a "compassion system"? You can use current events to acquaint the students with situations in which people have decided or must decide on the relative importance (significance, value, worth, etc.) of justice and compassion. (This, of course, is a rather philosophical concept for younger students. However, you may be surprised at their grasp of the ideas. It will, at least, familiarize them with the terms and open them to the concepts.)

Competition and Cooperation

At first glance the dichotomy between competition and cooperation seems much less philosophical and much more down to earth than the other choices discussed in this chapter. However, the differences between these two styles and the general approval given to competition in our society probably have a great deal to do with the escalation of conflict in general. Competition is deeply entrenched in the American character and has generally been seen as a virtue. Americans join teams, of course, but once on a team, they fight for positions or to make the "first string." The teams themselves are formed for the purposes of competition, of trying to be the best, of striving to win. These competitive adults want their children to compete also and to compete successfully, not just on teams but in school.

For a long time the move toward cooperative learning in the schools was seen as a threat to the excellence to be gained through competition. Now, since more and more companies in the United States are having their employees form work teams in the interest of greater production and higher profits, the attitude toward cooperative learning is gradually changing. Although cooperative learning in the classroom was certainly not invented or established for the purpose of resolving conflict, it has the potential for working that way.

For a long time the move toward cooperative learning in the schools was seen as a threat to the excellence to be gained through competition.

M. Lee Manning and Robert Lucking, writing in *The Clearing House*, emphasize the use of cooperative learning in multicultural classrooms as an aid to improving both multicultural relationships and student performance. They suggest that cooperative learning can be a perfect tool to integrate education and culture. (Manning and Lucking, 1993)

Erik Strommen, writing in *Electronic Learning,* suggests that cooperative learning implemented as a method to increase student success can be complemented by the use of computers which have the ability to facilitate open-ended, interactive educational experiences. Advances in technology and the nature of work in the future will necessitate social skills, critical thinking, teamwork in problem solving, and management of diversity—all of which are fostered by cooperative learning. He feels that it is vital for more teachers to begin using cooperative learning strategies. (Strommen, 1995)

Parents are becoming more aware of the necessity of helping their children de-emphasize competition.

Parents are becoming more aware of the necessity of helping their children de-emphasize competition. Writing in *Parenting,* Benjamin Spock warns parents that those who force their children into premature academic study or competitive sports may be causing psychological harm. (Spock, 1993) Carol Krucoff writes in *Parents Magazine* about helping kids to deal with competition by developing skills that help them cope with losing. (Krucoff, 1995) Roberta Israeloff, also writing in *Parents Magazine,* gives advice on how parents can help competitive children by lessening their own focus on competition. (Israeloff, 1996)

Students, too, can be given the opportunity to compare the ideas of cooperation and competition and decide when one or the other is appropriate. Give them a list of activities and ask them to decide which ones go with cooperation and which ones go with competition. Try words like football games, football teams, play rehearsals, tennis games, orchestra practice, chorus or choir, ice skating, committee work, family life, piloting a plane, racing cars, playing video games, and taking turns. Have the students give a rationale for each placement. Ask them which style they prefer—competition or cooperation. Why? Which one is more exciting? Which one has no winners or losers?

How to Start Cooperative Learning

The implementation of cooperative learning in the classroom will set the stage for using the tools of conflict resolution that will be presented in the next chapter. If you are a teacher who wants to begin using cooperative learning in your classroom, you should not only set the stage by creating an environment in which students feel free to talk but you should also put into motion a plan of classroom management that allows you to feel relaxed and comfortable with what is going on. Let your principal know what you are doing. Write letters to the parents and invite them to come in. Let everybody concerned know what to expect: a good cooperative learning classroom will be noisy and full of movement; everybody will be talking about what they are doing; the students will definitely not be sitting silently in straight rows. Distribute enough information about the method so that you will not be embarrassed by surprise visits from parents, other teachers, or administrators. Have stacks of photocopied explanatory materials on hand to pass out to uninformed and/or critical drop-in guests.

When selecting the members of your cooperative groups, be sure to create a mix of all four types in as many groups as possible.

Your personal goal should be to look calm and in control at all times, no matter what kind of chaos swirls around you. A secret weapon on your side is the *silent hand signal.* Simply raise your hand in the air and look around the room with an air of serene confidence. The first student who sees what you are doing should stop talking and raise his or her hand. Others should quickly follow until you can hear a pin drop in the room as everyone waits breathlessly to hear what you will say. This effect is worth all of the practice and rewards it will take to establish it. (Spend a lot of time practicing it at first; be lavish with your praise and generous with your rewards. After a while you may wish to practice and reward only intermittently to maintain the habit.)

Whether you are teaching very young students who are just giving up parallel play or older students who have been working independently for quite awhile, help them ease into cooperative learning by introducing them to partner activities first. Letting partners interview one another is a great way to get started. When you move into real group work, choose your groups carefully. While all young people are different, and certainly their abilities and skill levels can change, most students fit into at least one of these four categories:

- High Achievers
- Competent Achievers
- Special Needs Students
- English as a Second Language (ESL) Students

When selecting the members of your cooperative groups, be sure to create a mix of all four types in as many groups as possible. Also take into account gender, ethnicity, personality type, and learning style. For example, do not put all of your outgoing Latino boys with bodily-kinesthetic intelligence in the same group. Consult the next three pages for additional tips.

Components of Cooperative Learning

There are four basic components of cooperative learning. These components make the differences between cooperative learning and traditional group activities. Many of the group activities that you have used in the past can be adapted for cooperative learning by adjusting the activities to include the components listed below.

> There are four basic components of cooperative learning. These components make the differences between cooperative learning and traditional group activities.

1. **In cooperative learning all group members need to work together to accomplish the task.** No one is finished until the whole group is finished. The task or activity needs to be designed so that members are not each completing their own part but are working to complete one product together.

2. **Cooperative learning groups should be heterogeneous.** It is helpful to start by organizing groups so that there is a balance of abilities within and between groups. You may also wish to consider other variables when balancing groups.

3. **Cooperative learning activities need to be designed so that each student contributes to the group and individual group members can be assessed on their performances.** This can be accomplished by assigning each member a role that is essential to the completion of the task or activity. When input must be gathered from all of the members of the group, no one can go along for a free ride.

4. **Cooperative learning teams need to know the social as well as the academic objectives of a lesson.** Students need to know what they are expected to learn and how they are supposed to be working together to accomplish the learning. Students need to process or think and talk about how they worked on social skills as well as to evaluate how well their group worked on accomplishing the academic objective. Social skills are not something that students automatically know; these skills need to be taught.

The Teacher's Role During Cooperative Lessons

The teacher's role is quite different during cooperative lessons from what it is during teacher-directed lessons. The teacher has some important decisions to make prior to the lesson, but when the students are working in cooperative groups, the teacher's role is facilitator instead of trainer. When things are running smoothly, the teacher should circulate and observe how the teams are working.

Teachers may need to intervene in the following situations:

1. To get the group back on target if they are unsure of what to do.
2. To give immediate feedback to the group on how they are progressing with the task or activity.
3. To clarify something or to give further information to the whole class after observing a general difficulty or mastery.
4. To assist in the development of social skills through praise and group reflection.
5. To encourage or congratulate the group on how they are progressing with the task.

One caution for teachers is to avoid intervening if the group does not need assistance. Part of collaboration is learning how to discuss what comes next, to examine how the group is doing, and to decide when the group is finished. To successfully progress at this, students need time to work through the different stages and to solve their own problems.

The teacher's role is quite different during cooperative lessons from what it is during teacher-directed lessons.

Adapted from TCM Workshop Current Trends: Making Them Work, *Teacher Created Materials, 1991*

Student Roles

Teachers often find that using job assignments or roles helps students to know what part of the task or activity they are responsible for completing. It gives them specific information on what they need to do to help their teams.

Roles that work effectively:

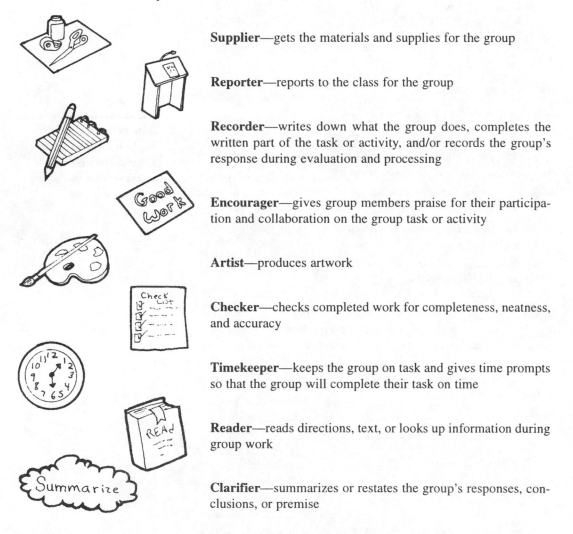

Supplier—gets the materials and supplies for the group

Reporter—reports to the class for the group

Recorder—writes down what the group does, completes the written part of the task or activity, and/or records the group's response during evaluation and processing

Encourager—gives group members praise for their participation and collaboration on the group task or activity

Artist—produces artwork

Checker—checks completed work for completeness, neatness, and accuracy

Timekeeper—keeps the group on task and gives time prompts so that the group will complete their task on time

Reader—reads directions, text, or looks up information during group work

Clarifier—summarizes or restates the group's responses, conclusions, or premise

The teacher needs to select specific roles for group work depending on the task or activity. Roles need to be taught and modeled for the class. After a period of experience with cooperative learning, specific roles may not be necessary each time for groups that work well together. In this case, groups will naturally divide up the task, with each group member doing what he or she likes or is especially capable of doing.

Drawing Conclusions

Once you have implemented cooperative learning groups in your classroom, ask your students to draw some conclusions about what they have learned.

Cooperation happens *within* a group. Competition happens *between* groups. Cooperation and competition can go on at the same time within teams and between teams, within classes and between classes, within schools and between schools, within political parties and between political parties, within cities and between cities, within states and between states, within countries and between countries, etc. For example, some students may compete with another class on a daily basis and yet cooperate with that same class when the whole school is involved in a project.

Students should now know what the differences are between cooperation and competition. What have they discovered about the relationship between these two ways of acting? Can they suggest any new ideas about how to motivate people to be cooperative?

What effect does the possibility of competition between groups have on the amount of cooperation within those groups? Have your students discuss this question. (Ask, for example, if they think that athletic teams work together better when they know a big game with another team is coming up or if the people in a country pull together and cooperate more effectively when they are confronted with the threat of war?)

Based on what your students have learned and discussed, ask them to think of a situation that would motivate the countries of the world to stop competing and start cooperating with one another. Have them suggest the titles of books, songs, and movies that have been based on this theme.

Review with your students the definitions of interpersonal and intrapersonal intelligences. Which learning style would a cooperative person be most likely to have? Which would a competitive person be most likely to have? (Be sure to tell them that it is possible for one person to have both of these intelligences and to be able to switch back and forth.)

Ask the students if they think that it is possible to develop another intelligence in themselves? How would they go about it? Would they like to be more cooperative or more competitive, or are they happy with themselves the way they are now?

Cooperation happens *within* a group. Competition happens *between* groups.

47

Making Appropriate Choices in Review

Take a look at what you have learned about making appropriate choices by applying the components to yourself and your students.

Rules and Self-Direction in Review

Would you rather follow the rules or be self-directed? Which is easier for you? Which is more satisfying to you? Are there ever times when it is wrong to follow the rules?

Fairness and Extenuating Circumstances in Review

Do you like things to be fair? What is fairness? What are extenuating circumstances? Is it hard or easy for you to make exceptions to the rules? Would you be glad if people made exceptions for you under special circumstances?

Justice and Compassion in Review

Is compassion an emotional reaction that you often have when you know that someone is troubled or suffering? Do you have a desire to help? Do you ever follow up on that desire and actually do something? Do you know people who are without compassion? How do you feel about them?

Competition and Cooperation in Review

Why have people in the United States been apprehensive about the effects of cooperative learning in the classroom? What new development in American business has made some people change their minds? What are some of the benefits of cooperative learning and cooperation in general? Have you tried cooperative learning in your classroom? With what results?

Using Techniques for Conflict Resolution

The Real Tools

Through the process of developing self-concepts, growing in social awareness, acquiring communication skills, developing respect and empathy, and learning to make appropriate choices, the groundwork has been laid for learning to use the actual tools of conflict resolution. There are many ways to approach conflict resolution and many names for each of the tools. The ones we will consider here are **assertiveness**, **negotiation**, **compromise**, and **mediation**.

Assertiveness

Webster's (1994) defines assertiveness as the ability to be positive or confident in a persistent way. Young people would probably call it the ability to stick up for themselves. However it is defined and whatever it is called, assertiveness is characterized by many of the skills and attitudes that have already been discussed in this book. Assertiveness is based on respect (respect and empathy) for

Webster's (1994) defines assertiveness as the ability to be positive or confident in a persistent way.

oneself (self-concept) and for others (social awareness). It depends on the ability to give clear oral messages (communication skills). In addition, assertiveness is "persistent," which students can think of as "stubborn in a polite way."

Difficult at All Ages

It is hard to be assertive. Many adults take classes in "Assertiveness Training" to learn how to do it. Some of these adults found that they could not say "no" to requests from other people. Some of them realized that they always reacted with anger to situations that could have been handled assertively. When you are assertive, you do not submit (become passive) and you do not become angry (become aggressive). Furthermore, you put yourself in a good position to negotiate and compromise, which are ways of reaching an agreement that we will be learning more about.

Three Types of Reaction

Students should learn about three types of reactive behavior—passive, aggressive, and assertive—and the relationship among them. Very briefly, a *passive* person gives in, an *aggressive* person becomes angry, and an *assertive* person sticks up for himself or herself. Various activities are appropriate for teaching these behaviors at different grade levels.

Teaching Assertiveness to Very Young Children

Even very young students need to be given some acceptable and practical techniques for using assertive behavior. Without any help in or support for acting another way, small children, like adults, are more apt to give in (use passive behavior) or become angry (use aggressive behavior). A workable approach at the kindergarten or first grade level is to pick one or two specific behaviors and then give the students some assertiveness tools and the training to use these tools. The two behaviors might be *taking turns* and *protecting personal property.*

At least some of the behaviors routinely expected from young children make it hard for them to be assertive. We caution students to give others their turns ("Let Johnny use the ball now." "It's Maria's turn to ride the tricycle."), but we do not always remember to make sure that they get their turns. We spend a lot of time in school teaching students to share with others ("Please share these crayons at your table." "Roberto's mother sent cookies for him to share with the class."), and then we often become upset because they do not respect one another's private possessions.

50

"It's My Turn!"

You can solve the taking-turns problem by providing signs that designate "Taking-Turns" activities, timers for each activity, and instructions in how to use them. Even though children at this age may not be reading, if you explain the signs and read them aloud often enough, your students will remember what they say. The signs are simply there to back up the person who is learning to stand up for herself or himself. You might choose to put a sign that says "This Is a Taking-Turns Activity" next to a particularly popular puzzle or over your painting easels. Also post "Rules for Taking Turns" and a sign that says "One Turn = _____Minutes."

During your circle time, tell your students that you are going to show them how to use the signs. First, display the signs and read them all out loud. Ask the students to point them out: Which sign says "This Is a Taking-Turns Activity"? Which sign tells the rules? Which sign tells how to set the timer? Pass the timers around and let all of the students have a turn to set one. Then ask two students to demonstrate.

Have one of the students go to the puzzle table and check the sign that tells how long a turn should be. Have that student set the timer and begin to play with the puzzle. Ask the other student to come up and start to move the puzzle pieces around. Tell the student who got there first to point to the sign and say, "This is a taking-turns activity. Remember the rules." Have everyone practice making this assertive statement. Repeat the whole scenario until everyone has had a chance to role-play and make the assertive statement.

Put your sets of signs up in different places around the room where you have activities in which students should take turns. Remind your students that they can get you if they need help. They can also help each other remember what the signs say.

Decide, based on your own situation and group of students, whether or not you want to call attention to the behaviors that are being replaced by this assertive approach. You could say, "Sometimes students think they can't stick up for themselves when someone tries to take an unfair turn. Sometimes students become very angry. These signs and words will help you to stand up for yourself without becoming angry."

Sample Rules for Taking Turns

These rules will work with the activity described above.

> Decide, based on your own situation and group of students, whether or not you want to call attention to the behaviors that are being replaced by this assertive approach.

1. If someone is using the activity, wait quietly until the timer dings.

2. Give the person time to clean up.

3. When it is your turn, check the sign that tells how many minutes in a turn.

4. Set the timer.

5. Take your turn.

"This Is Mine!"

Children often need help and support in protecting their rights to their own property. A child, as well as an adult, should be able to bring something of his or her own to school without being expected to share it. Imagine how you, if you are a female teacher, would feel if the principal said to you, "What a great new laptop! Be sure to share it with the other teachers during your break." Or, imagine how you would feel as a male teacher if another teacher said to the principal, "Bob won't let me hold his new camera," and the principal said to you, "Oh Bob, don't be so selfish!" We do this sort of thing to children all of the time. We expect them to share their cherished possessions with anyone who asks, and yet we are horrified if they pick up something that is not their own. Then we call it stealing.

In order to support the students' rights to have their own property respected, to remind them to respect the property of others, and because small children find it hard to stick up for themselves, make or buy buttons or stickers (which can be made with pieces of paper and double sided tape) that say "This Is Mine!" Tell the students that they can use these to tell other people to leave their things alone. Be sure to remind them that they must give other people's things the same respect. Show them where to find the buttons or stickers and how to put their names on them. Give them an assertive statement to use if someone picks up something that is theirs. Have them say, "This is mine. Please look at the sticker."

Teaching Assertiveness in the Elementary Grades

Students in the elementary grades need practice in making assertive statements. A workable approach at this level is to give the students a formula modeled on the feeling messages that they have already learned and practiced. Tell the students that if they remember how to send an "I" message, they already know how to make an assertive statement.

A child, as well as an adult, should be able to bring something of his or her own to school without being expected to share it.

52

Review the three kinds of reactive behavior with your students. Then have the students role-play a variety of situations, giving each kind of reaction. The following are two examples:

Situation: Pretend that you have gone to the classroom library and picked out a book. When you come back and sit down at your desk, the person next to you grabs the book and starts to read it. What will you do?

Responses: Don't say anything. Go and get another book. *(Passive)*

Grab the book back and slam it down on your desk. *(Aggressive)*

Say, "I would like to have my book. Please go and get your own." *(Assertive)*

Situation: A friend of yours is in charge of a committee that collects paper and cans to be recycled. He wants you to join the committee which meets every Saturday morning from 8 a.m. until noon. You have soccer practice from 1:00 p.m. until 4:00 P.M., and your mother also expects you to do some chores for her on Saturdays. You really don't want to be on the recycling team, but your friend is putting a lot of pressure on you and you know his feelings will be hurt if you refuse.

Responses: Sure. I'll be there, but I have to leave in time for practice. *(Passive)*

Stop bugging me! I don't want to be on your stupid committee! *(Aggressive)*

I'm sorry, but I can't be there. My Saturdays are already full. *(Assertive)*

Things to notice:

◆ An assertive statement is polite, but it is also honest.
◆ An assertive statement shows self-respect as well as respect for the other person.

Role-playing is very effective. However, no matter how much you have your students role-play, this kind of assertive behavior will only work, especially at this grade level, if you have established an environment of self-esteem, trust, and support in your classroom. Be on the lookout for students who need help with the responses they get from the classmates to whom they make their assertive statements. Check on these things: Did the people the

> **An assertive statement shows self-respect as well as respect for the other person.**

speaker addressed listen? How could the speaker tell? What did the people the speaker spoke to say or do? Were the assertive students satisfied with the results they got? Why or why not? (Assure them that the next parts of conflict resolution—negotiation and compromise—will help solve these problems.)

Teaching Assertiveness in the Upper Grades

In addition to all of the other information about assertiveness, students in the upper grades need to know that there are some situations when being safe is much more important than being either honest or polite and when keeping their self-respect is more important than showing respect for another person. These are situations in which they are being asked to do things that are dangerous or against the law. In these cases, although they will not want to be passive or aggressive, their assertiveness will need to be more unequivocal; that is, they should make it clear that there are no other choices.

There are many ways to handle extreme situations:

◆ Make a clear "I" statement. (Say what you think and feel.)

◆ Put the responsibility somewhere else. (For example, blame your parents.)

◆ Use the "broken record" technique. (Say the same thing over and over.)

◆ Walk (or run) away. (Leave the situation.)

◆ Report it. (Get away and tell an adult.)

Give your students a sample situation and ask them to create responses. (A sample situation and responses are given below.) Then make up or have them make up more situations to respond to.

Situation: A friend of yours has agreed to fight someone after school in the park. He wants you to come with him. The person he is going to fight belongs to a gang. On top of that, your school has strict rules about fights that include suspension for anyone who is even watching. You are afraid for him, but you are even more afraid for yourself.

Clear statement: I think it's a bad idea. I won't be there.

Responsibility: My mother would ground me forever if I got suspended!

Broken record: No, no, no, no . . . .

Walk away: (Just go home after school.)

Report it: (Tell someone in authority what is going to happen.)

Negotiation

Learning to be assertive is only the first part of managing conflict. If this approach is not met with immediate success, students need to know what to do next. Negotiation, or bargaining, is the next step in this process, and students will need a great deal of coaching to go on to this new level.

Helping Very Young Students to Understand Negotiation

In the process of negotiation, two (or more) sides offer plans and then work their way toward an agreement through a bargaining process. Basic to this approach, of course, is having a plan to offer. Brainstorming is one way of generating plans, and even very young children can learn to brainstorm. This may be as far as you will want to go in teaching negotiation for children in kindergarten and first grade.

Think of a problem you would like to solve in your classroom. For example, you could tell your students that you have noticed that they are crowding at the door too much when they line up for lunch. Explain that this can be dangerous because someone could be pushed and get hurt. It is really necessary to think of a way to solve this problem. (You can use your own problem instead, of course.)

Before listening to any ideas, explain that you are going to teach them how to do something called *brainstorming*. Brainstorming is a process in which all ideas are initially accepted. The ideas are all written down without trying to decide if they are good or bad. After all of the ideas have been written down, the group can talk about which ones might work the best.

Have your students give ideas while you write them on the chalkboard. If you are using the lunch line problem, you might come up with results similar to the following:

1. Let one person at a time go to lunch.
2. Appoint a line monitor.
3. Pushers go to lunch late.
4. Draw lines for people to stand on.
5. Make a nice line.
6. Pushers go to the end of the line.

> In the process of negotiation, two (or more) sides offer plans and then work their way toward an agreement through a bargaining process.

Discuss the ideas. State the ideal outcome: Everybody can line up for lunch without pushing.

◆ Number 5 would be the best solution. It would mean that we all could follow the rules without help.

◆ Number 2 would be the next best solution. The monitor could have people stand on lines and send pushers to the end of the line. (This would also incorporate numbers 4 and 6.)

◆ Numbers 1 and 3 are last resorts—things we can do if none of the other plans work.

Ask your students which plan they would like to try first. After a week, have them decide if the plan they chose is working. Do they want to keep using it, or is it time to choose another plan?

Negotiation in the Elementary and Upper Grades

Older students can apply negotiation skills to conflict situations. Tell the students that negotiation is a bargaining process that helps people on opposite sides of an issue reach an agreement. The first step in negotiation is for each side to state its demands or tell what it wants. Each side has a plan. In real bargaining situations, these plans usually contain extra things that the people do not really care about. They are then prepared to give up these things in exchange for things that the other side will give up. (This prepares them for the next step, compromise.)

Try an activity sheet like this one:

Negotiation Activity Sheet

Directions: Work with your group to write a plan for each side in the following situation. Try to include some features that you would be willing to give up.

Situation

Your class is planning a graduation party that will cost $10.00 per student. The school district usually pays for this party, but money is short this year so the teacher has suggested that each student pay his or her own way. The students who cannot bring $10.00 think that the school district should pay anyway. A few students who are trying to be helpful suggest collecting and redeeming recyclables to raise the money.

In favor of the school district paying:

_____

_____

_____

In favor of students paying their own way:

_____

_____

_____

In favor of raising money with recyclables:

_____

_____

_____

Have the students think of additional problems, with two or more possible solutions, that face them individually or as a class. Divide the class into groups to write out plans for negotiation. Ask them to try to include demands that they would be willing to give up. (Or, make up more problems and have them take opposing sides.)

Negotiation and Feelings

People often have strong feelings about the plans that they offer for the purposes of negotiations. While they may not always express these feelings, it helps to be able to acknowledge them and to realize that the people on the other side of the negotiation table may have strong feelings too. Have your students work in small groups to consider the plans that they made up for situations. Ask them to pick a situation and then to speculate about the feelings of the people who might have taken the various sides in their plans. Who would feel the most strongly about each of the plans? Come back to the large group to compare and discuss the results. Ask the students questions such as these: How did you go about deciding on the feelings? Did you base your ideas on how you would have felt yourself or on how someone you know might have felt?

Compromise

When people compromise, they meet each other in the middle. Each side may give a little (hopefully, what they care the least about) to get a little (hopefully, what they care the most about). In a compromise situation, it is almost impossible for everyone to be *totally* happy.

Helping Very Young Students to Understand Compromise

Below is a situation which offers a perfect opportunity for teaching compromise:

Pham: I want to play with the trains now by myself!

Nick: I want to play with the trains now by myself!

Teacher: What is the most important part of playing with the trains—doing it *now* or doing it *by yourself*? If playing *now* is the most important, you can play together. If playing *by yourself* is the most important, you can take turns with the timer.

Ask the students what they could do in these cases:

Student #1: I want you to read *The Very Hungry Caterpillar.*

Student #2: I want you to read *The Very Quiet Cricket.*

(Read one book and then the other.)

> **When people compromise, they meet each other in the middle.**

Student #1: I want to use the ABC puzzle first.

Student #2: I want to use the ABC puzzle first.

(Use another puzzle while you wait to take turns with the ABC puzzle.)

Student #1: I want to play with the yellow ball.

Student #2: I want to play with the yellow ball too.

(Play together, take turns with the yellow ball, or use another ball.)

Ask the students to tell you when they notice a situation that requires a compromise. Have them tell you what each person wants and what their choices are.

Compromise in the Elementary and Upper Grades

Reaching agreements about negotiation plans is a big part of using and understanding compromise. Have the students work in small groups, using the negotiation plans they made, to come up with compromise ideas that might be acceptable to all of the sides. If you used the negotiation activity sheet dealing with the issue of the graduation party, they can start by writing a compromise plan for that problem and then go on to the other situations they worked on.

The situations explored so far have dealt with circumstances that were important to a number of people. However, compromises take place in everyday circumstances as well as in major situations. Almost every time someone expresses a feeling with an "I" message and someone else uses active listening to receive the message, there is an opportunity for compromise in the response.

If you go all the way through the formulas, you will finally reach the place where compromise can take place:

1st person: I can't stand it when you look at my answers! I want you to quit it. *("I" message)*

2nd person: I understand that you get mad when you think I look at your answers, and you want me to quit. *(active listening restated to show comprehension)*

But look at it from my side. Your paper is right there in front of me. I wish you would cover it up or something. *(other perspective/"I" message)*

1st person: Okay. I'll move it to the other side of my desk. *(compromise response)*

2nd person: And I'll try not to look at it. *(compromise response)*

Have the students try acting out these first person "I" statements all the way to compromises:

- ◆ I'm sorry that you got into trouble when George threw that paper airplane. I wish you'd let me tell the teacher what really happened.
- ◆ I don't want to walk home with you after school. I want you to stop asking me.
- ◆ I don't believe your dog ate your homework. I think you should tell the truth.

Mediation

The role of mediation in the area of conflict resolution has two distinct components. One part consists of training students to help one another deal with conflict situations. The other part deals with the students' right to ask for help both from their peers and from adults.

In our efforts to teach children not to be tattletales, we very often make them feel that it is wrong to ask for help from an adult. Older students can be taught to turn to a peer mediator for help; however, all children need to know that teachers and other adults are still available to assist in solving problems. If the students have learned to use "I" messages, listen actively, speak assertively, offer plans for solutions, and compromise, there will not be as much of a need for mediation but there will certainly still be some.

Students of all ages need to be protected from bullies. The bully needs to be helped too. More and more research being done in this area shows that bullying is a very serious problem that, left untreated, can result in serious consequences later in school and in adult life.

Bullies and their victims can be identified early on by their behaviors and personality characteristics. An excellent and concise overview of both personality types can be found in *Teaching Students to Get Along* by Lee Canter and Katia Petersen. Both personality types can be helped by activities that build their self-esteem. (Canter and Petersen, 1995)

Mediation and Very Young Children

During your circle time, ask your students to define the word *bully*. Do they know any bullies? Has anyone ever bullied them? Discuss the situations that are reported.

More and more research being done in this area shows that bullying is a very serious problem that, left untreated, can result in serious consequences later in school and in adult life.

Build self-esteem by having your students exchange compliments during circle time. Ask them to call each other by name and say one nice thing when called upon. ("Mary, I like the picture you painted.") Hand out "Compliment Cards" on a regular basis. These can be simple hand-printed cards that say things like "Great Work!" or "WOW!" or you can find more elaborate cards that can be duplicated in many teacher resource books.

Be sure to tell your students that they are supposed to tell you or another adult when someone is being a bully. This is not tattling. It is something you need to know. If the problem seems to be serious, get help right away from your school psychologist or guidance counselor and deal with the situation as quickly as possible.

Mediation and the Elementary School Student

Elementary school students can be taught the basics of peer mediation; however, all children need to know that the teacher is still available to assist in solving problems and to protect them in dangerous situations.

At this age, try to increase student awareness. Introduce the idea of "Mediation Requests," printed slips that a student can drop into a "Mediation Request Box" in order to ask for help.

Build your students' self-esteems with activities that showcase their positive qualities. Choosing a "Student of the Week" helps many students to see both themselves and others as unique and special. Take pictures of the students and help them fill out forms telling something about themselves. Post these in a prominent place in the classroom. (See the sample "Student of the Week" form on the next page.)

Introduce the idea of peer mediation. If a program of this type is available in your school, encourage your students to take part in it. Students in many schools are forming groups with names like Peacemakers, Peace Patrol, SAVE (Students Against Violence Everywhere), and so on. If there is no mediation program already in place in your school, you may want to start a mini-program in your own classroom. Many programs are available to help you. Some of them are listed at the end of this book.

Build your students' self-esteems with activities that showcase their positive qualities.

Student of the Week

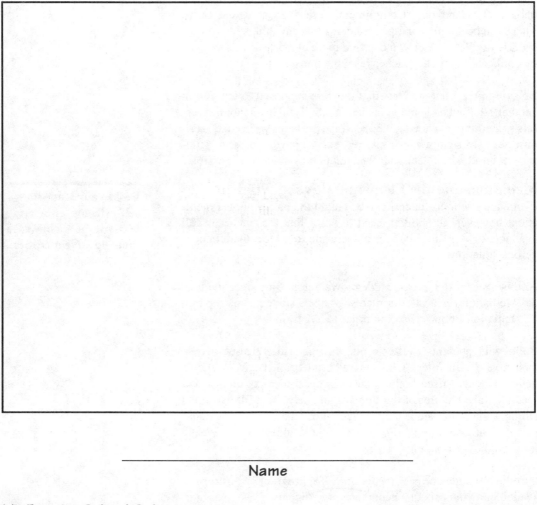

_____
Name

My Favorite School Subject: _____

My Favorite Sport: _____

My Favorite Television Show: _____

My Favorite Video Game: _____

My Favorite Book: _____

Mediation and the Upper Grade Student

Tell your students that while they can always ask you for help, they are now going to learn to help each other. Give them information about the groups that exist in many other schools. Have them write letters asking for information. If possible, join any peer mediation program that is already in place in your school. If none exists, your plan can begin in your own classroom. If it is successful and helpful to the students, they may want to present it to the school and teach others how to do it. Tell them that they may help any classmate who wants help and that you will make a script available for them to use. Remind them that you will always be available for backup.

Becoming part of the peer mediation team can be a great self-esteem booster for your students. You can extend this program to all of your students or have special rules and qualifications for the job. There is something to be said for both approaches. Meeting special requirements is an extra boost for kids. They can be looked up to by others and so on. However, helping others, even if you are not perfect yourself, can give you an added incentive to try. This is entirely up to you and will probably depend on the makeup of your current group of students and your educational philosophy.

> **Becoming part of the peer mediation team can be a great self-esteem booster for your students.**

Still another approach is to have the responsibility for being a peer mediator rotate around the classroom, perhaps six students a week. They can wear peer mediator badges and take a pledge at the beginning of their week. Use this pledge or compose one of your own.

Peer Mediator Pledge

I promise to be ready and willing to help anyone who asks for help.

I will be polite and respectful to the people whom I help.

I will follow the Peer Mediation Script.

I will ask the teacher for help, if necessary.

Note: The Peer Mediation Script is on page 65.

Get ready by reviewing with your students the lessons dealing with sending information with "I" messages, receiving information with active listening, and responding to information with the appropriate behavior. Run through a variety of situations, letting your students play the parts of the peer mediators. Use the formula on the next page.

Peer Mediation Example

Situation: A visibly upset student (let's call her Dina) comes into the classroom after lunch.

Peer Mediator: Do you need help, Dina?

Dina: Frank makes me sick!

Peer Mediator: Can you tell me what is wrong by using an "I" message?

Dina: I feel angry and disgusted when Frank calls me names. I want him to stop.

Peer Mediator: Frank, please come and talk to us. Did you hear Dina?

Frank: Yeah.

Peer Mediator: Please use active listening to tell us what Dina said.

Frank: Dina said she feels angry and disgusted when I call her names, and she wants me to stop.

Peer Mediator: Now tell us that in your own words.

Frank: Dina wants me to stop calling her names because it really makes her mad.

Peer Mediator: Is that right, Dina?

Dina: Yes.

Peer Mediator: Can you say anything to make Dina feel better, Frank?

Frank: Sorry, Dina.

Peer Mediator: Is there anything that you can do to make Dina feel better?

Frank: I can stop calling her names.

Peer Mediator: Do you feel okay about that, Dina?

Dina: Yes. Thank you.

Peer Mediator: That was good communication!

Peer Mediator Script

Mediator Directions: In the case of a conflict, use this script to guide a conversation between the two opposing parties. The blank lines are for the students' names and their responses.

Peer Mediator: Do you need help, _____ ?

First Person's Response: _____

Peer Mediator: Can you tell me what is wrong by using an "I" message?

First Person's Response: _____

Peer Mediator: _____ , please come and talk to us. Did you hear _____ ?

Second Person's Response: _____

Peer Mediator: Please use active listening to tell us what _____ said.

Second Person's Response: _____

Peer Mediator: Now tell us that in your own words.

Second Person's Response: _____

Peer Mediator: Is that right, _____ ?

First Person's Response: _____

Peer Mediator: Can you say anything to make _____ feel better?

Second Person's Response: _____

Peer Mediator: Is there anything that you can do to make _____ feel better?

Second Person's Response: _____

Peer Mediator: Do you feel okay about that, _____ ?

First Person's Response: _____

Peer Mediator: That was good communication!

Provide additional support for the students who need adult help in dealing with a conflict situation by formalizing your mediation request program. Remind them that they are supposed to tell you or another adult when someone is being a bully. (See information about bullies on page 60.) Make sure that the students know that reporting a bully is not tattling. It is never tattling to report any situation that involves danger or abuse, whether physical or emotional.

Make a Help Box (like a suggestion box) for your classroom and place a stack of mediation requests next to it. Preserve the security of the box by keeping it on your desk. Discuss some situations that would warrant the use of a mediation request and let the students know that they can request help for someone else as well as for themselves.

Be sensitive to the needs of your students and, if you promise confidentiality, be sure to keep your word.

Be aware that the peer culture of the pre-adolescent and adolescent is not conducive to "telling on" people, even when there is real danger or abuse. Be sensitive to the needs of your students and if you promise confidentiality, be sure to keep your word.

Provide many self-esteem building opportunities in your classroom. Some good ones are the following:

◆ classroom jobs that highlight responsibility
◆ creative projects that can be recognized
◆ cross-age tutoring to help younger students
◆ classroom offices with real duties
◆ recognition of effort as well as grades

Your peer mediation program can be considered successful if (1) you do not need to use it, (2) students are not afraid to use it, or (3) its use is effective in resolving conflicts.

Other Views of Conflict Management

As noted at the beginning of this chapter, there are many ways of approaching the management of conflict and many names for the various steps. Articles about conflict management appear in the most unlikely places. In a column called "Compassionate Living," from *The Animals' Agenda,* Victoria Moran writes about a four-step process of conflict resolution that involves finding a time to talk, planning the context, talking it out, and making a deal. (Moran, 1992) Sandra Arbetter, writing in *Current Health 2,* lists five steps for resolving conflict: identifying the problem, finding solutions, selecting the best solution, acting on the solution, and following through. (Arbetter, 1991) In 1992, *Working Mother* devoted part of an issue to conflict management with articles that focused on conflict management techniques for preschoolers (Conrad, 1992) and teenagers (Cosell, 1992). "Through the Years," a regular department of *Sesame Street Parents* edited by Katherine Ross, recently ran a series of short pieces by various authorities, detailing the ways in which children can be helped to cope with normal stages of anger from birth to age eleven. (Ross, 1996) In *Instructor,* where one would expect to find such an article, Meg Bozzone offers ten tips for conflict resolution, including the establishment of a "peaceable" classroom community. (Bozzone, 1994)

In *The Friendly Classroom for a Small Planet* the authors have provided an abundance of activities based on recognition, affirmation, communication, and cooperation, both to establish the environment for effective conflict management and to create what are called win-win situations for students. The book also contains an extensive list of the branches of the Children's Creative Response to Conflict Program (CCRC) and many related resources, all with addresses and many with telephone numbers. A new edition of this book is being prepared and will be out soon. (Prutzman, et al., 1988)

Barbara Porro's book *Talk It Out: Conflict Resolution in the Elementary Classroom* offers step-by-step advice for building a program of conflict resolution through peer interaction and mediation. She includes lesson plans and detailed scripts for using "I" messages and active listening, and she adds a very structured "Cooling Off" element to her method. (Porro, 1996)

Teaching Students to Get Along by Lee Canter and Katia Petersen includes the following sections in Chapter 6—"Teaching Skills for Responding to Conflict":

◆ Understanding the Escalation of Conflict
◆ Learning Assertiveness Skills
◆ Learning to "Stop, Think and Act"
◆ Learning Negotiation Skills

Their book also contains the excellent materials on bullies mentioned earlier. This information can be found in Chapter 7, "Standing Up to Bullying Behavior." (Canter and Petersen, 1995)

There are also many, many exemplary programs in individual schools and school districts around the country. An article in the *Los Angeles Times* recently told the story of a program called For Young Improvers (FYI) which has been in operation for two years at St. Thomas the Apostle School in Los Angeles. This peer mediation program—which teaches values such as trust, honesty, respect, and teamwork—culminated its year with a production of *Godspell*. This play and the FYI program have changed lives, according to principal Ted Horn. The school itself, located in one of Los Angeles' poorer areas, has been designated a National Blue Ribbon School of Excellence by President Clinton. Two teachers have been named teachers of the year by the Education Consortium of Central Los Angeles. In addition, Joseph Walsh, the director of *Godspell* who used to perform on Broadway and now teaches kindergarten, received a national award for first-year teachers. (Noriyuki, 1996)

The state of New Jersey's School Based Youth Services program is a school and community effort to provide conflict management services to young people. (Power, 1992) Schools in western New York are training students and staff in peer mediation skills. (Morse and Andrea, 1994) In fact, Janet Carr, writing in *Good Housekeeping,* reports that approximately 5,000 conflict resolution programs are in operation in public and private schools in the United States, according to the National Association for Mediation in Education (NAME). (Carr, 1994)

Using Techniques for Conflict Resolution Review
Take a look at what you have learned about using techniques for conflict resolution by applying the components to yourself and your students.

Assertiveness in Review
Are you able to stick up for yourself without becoming passive or aggressive? Do you know that you have a right to finish your turn and the right to protect your own property? Can you send an assertive "I" message? Do you know how to deal with extreme situations?

Negotiation in Review
Do you know how to brainstorm ideas for a negotiation plan? Do you know how to make a plan that allows room for compromising? Can you recognize strong feelings on both sides of the negotiation table?

Approximately 5,000 conflict resolution programs are in operation in public and private schools in the United States.

Compromise in Review

Can you meet someone in the middle? Can you give a little to get a little? Can you extend communication from an "I" message all the way to a compromise statement? Are you aware that a compromise can never make everybody *totally* happy?

Mediation in Review

Do you know what a bully is? Do you realize that it is always all right to ask for help ("tell on" someone) in situations that are dangerous or abusive? What do you know about peer mediation? Are you able to help others through the mediation process?

Other Views of Conflict Management in Review

There are many sources to choose from in starting conflict management and/or peer mediation programs in your classroom or in your school. You can use a single program as a whole or mix and match elements of different programs to suit your own style and the needs of your student community. Whatever you choose to do, whether it is on a small or large scale, you will be able to find groups to support your efforts and applaud your successes.

Teaching Peace

The Ultimate Goal
The ultimate goal of conflict resolution is peace. All of the concepts that have been discussed, all of the skills that have been practiced, were designed to lead to just one end—peace . . . peace in the classroom, peace in the school, peace in the neighborhood, and peace in general.

Another Way to Get There
There are people—educators and psychologists—who feel that we are going about the peace process backwards and that we should focus on peace from the very beginning rather than making an issue of conflict. Colman McCarthy, writing in the *National Catholic Reporter,* goes so far as to suggest adding an office of peace education to the United States Department of Education.

In an article entitled, "Needed: Teaching Peace Literacy by Numbers," McCarthy describes a society in which math is not taught in the schools. The citizens are helpless to manage their everyday lives. No one knows what the amount of his or her next paycheck should be. No one knows who won or lost a sporting event because scores cannot be kept. A few people in this hypothetical society have picked up math on their own, but they are considered eccentrics. Teachers who try to slip in some math instruction are reported to the school board as radicals.

"That's about where we are regarding the teaching of . . . peace-making," concludes McCarthy. McCarthy envisions his proposed office of peace education as a resource center, a source for curriculum development, and a clearinghouse for information about the successful peace programs operating around the country. (McCarthy, 1992)

More Peace Teaching

While McCarthy's plan is probably a utopian dream, considering it is occasionally suggested to get rid of the whole Department of Education, many other people are also thinking along the same lines about teaching peace. The winning essay in the North American Essay Contest, "Teaching Peace" by Kristen Porter, was published in *The Humanist.* The theme of this essay is that families and schools must teach peace to the children since television and the movies often concentrate on teaching war. She cites some appalling statistics about the number of hours children spend absorbing information about war and war toys. (Porter, 1992) The attempt to teach peace through cooperative rather than competitive board games was reported by Erica Franklin in *American Health: Fitness of Body and Mind* in an article titled "Kinder, Gentler Toys: New Board Games Teach Cooperation and Social Values." (Franklin, 1990)

Meanwhile, back in school, the peace programs are still being implemented. In an article titled "Playground Peace Talk" that appeared in *Parenting,* Diane Pruffer describes the successful results of peer mediation programs in general. She makes the interesting point that these programs have now existed for over ten years. (Pruffer, 1992) Mary Beth Spann writes in *Instructor* about the use of puppets to ease conflict in the classroom. In an article titled "Make Peace-Keeping Playful," she gives a rationale for using puppets, tips for getting ready, and four steps for resolving conflict with puppet play. The steps are (1) defining the dispute, (2) brainstorming solutions, (3) picking a strategy, and (4) providing time for follow-up. (Spann, 1994)

In September of 1996, *Educational Leadership* devoted an entire issue to "Creating a Climate for Learning" with article after article devoted to methods for teaching peace. One of these articles, "The Road to Peace in Our Schools" by Linda Lantieri with Janet Patti, details the growth of the Resolving Conflict

Puppets can be used to ease conflict in the elementary classroom.

Creatively Program (RCCP). The program began in 1985 in three schools in Brooklyn. It is now operating in eight school systems in five states and serves about 150,000 students. Its unique contribution to conflict resolution and peer mediation is the "peaceable schools" model. The program requires a long-term commitment of at least five years and includes a K–12 curriculum, professional development for teachers, student-led mediation, administrator training, and parent education. The experiences of the people involved in the program, together with independent studies by several groups of outside evaluators, have found that the program works. Students feel safe and empowered, and learning is enhanced. (Lantieri and Patti, 1996)

Peace for the Children

For the children themselves, get *The Big Book for Peace*, an anthology of stories, pictures, and poems about peace. The literature pieces were created especially for this book by a collection of celebrated authors and illustrators who have arranged to have their royalties, along with the publisher's income from the book, donated to a selection of peace organizations. (Durrell and Sachs, 1990)

Resources for Teaching Peace

Center for Conflict Resolution
200 N. Michigan Avenue, Suite 500
Chicago, IL 60601

The Center offers information and materials about the promotion of conflict resolution and peer mediation for children.

CCRC (Children's Creative Response to Conflict)
P.O. Box 271
Nyack, NY 10960
Phone: (914) 353-1796 FAX: (914) 358-4924

Children's Creative Response to Conflict presents many kinds of teacher training programs throughout the world. As an extension of their standard workshops and courses, they will custom design workshops to meet a group's time and theme requirements. Their handbook, *The Friendly Classroom for a Small Planet* by Priscilla Prutzman et al., is a wonderful resource. In addition to many creative lesson plans and ideas, it lists dozens of regional CCRC branches and related programs. Also available are a newsletter, *Sharing Space*, a literature service featuring books and articles, and a video describing the CCRC program.

The Lion and the Lamb Peace Arts Center
Bluffton College
Bluffton, OH 45817

Information and materials about the promotion of peace and international understanding through the arts and literature for children are available.

NAME (The National Association for Mediation in Education)
205 Hampshire House
Box 33635
University of Massachusetts
Amherst, MA 01003
Phone: (413) 545-2462

Information and materials about the promotion of conflict resolution and peer mediation for children are available.

Sunburst Communications
101 Castleton Street
P.O. Box 40
Pleasantville, NY 10570-9807
Phone: 1-800-431-1934
FAX: (914) 769-2109

Sunburst Communications offers videos, games, newsletters, and posters for grades K–12 on various subjects of guidance and health. They offer several videos specifically on conflict resolution. Request a catalog for more details about their products.

References

Adelson, J. (1996, February). Down with self-esteem. Commentary, 101 (2), 34–38.

Arbetter, S. (1991, September). Resolving conflict step by step. Current Health 2, 18 (1), 14–15.

Bell, A. (1996, March). The name game. Teen Magazine, 40 (3), 104–106.

Blumenthal, R. (1996, September). Tap your child's special strengths. Family Circle, 109 (12), 86–89.

Bower, B. (1993, May). Gender paths wind toward self-esteem. Science News, 143 (20), 308.

Bowser, J. (1993, January). Structuring the middle-school classroom for spoken language. English Journal, 82 (1), 38–41.

Boyles, D. (1996, October). Your name here. Men's Health, 11 (8), 56–57.

Bozzone, M. (1994, July-August). Spend less time refereeing and more time teaching: 10 tips for developing an effective conflict-resolution program. Instructor, 104 (1), 86–89.

Canter, L., and Petersen, K. (1995). Teaching students to get along. Santa Monica, CA: Lee Canter & Associates.

Carr, J. (1994, September). Learning to get along. Good Housekeeping, 219 (3), 177–178.

Conrad, E. (1992, January). Preschool report. Working Mother, 15 (1), 58–59.

Corbett, C. (1995, June). The winner within: A hands-on-guide to healthy self-esteem. Essence, 26 (2), 65–69.

Cosell, H. (1992, January). Tweens. Working Mother, 15 (1), 68.

Durrell, A., and Sachs, M. (Eds.). (1990). The big book for peace. New York: Dutton Children's Books.

Dwyer, V. (1993, February). Eye of the beholder: Young women have self-image problems. Maclean's, 106 (8), 46–47.

Faber, A., and Mazlish, E. (1995). How to talk so kids can learn. New York: Rawson Associates.

Ferguson, A. (1995, June). I'm terrific, you're terrific. Washingtonian, 30 (9), 43–48.

Franklin, E. (1990, July-August). Kinder, gentler toys: New board games teach cooperation and social values. American Health: Fitness of Body and Mind, 9 (6), 89.

Gardner, H. (1983). Frames of mind: The Theory of multiple intelligences. New York: Basic Books.

Gardner, H. (1993). Multiple intelligences: The theory in practice. New York: Basic Books.

Goldberg, C. (1995, October). This is me? The New York Times Magazine, page 56 (col. 1), 20 col. in.

Goodall, J. (1995, December). Message from Jane Goodall. National Geographic, 188 (6), 129.

Israeloff, R. (1996, August). "I got a billion trillion zillion!": How children use one-upmanship to build confidence. Parents Magazine, 71 (8), 138–140.

Johnson, K. (1992, February). "Objective" news reporting can poison young black minds. Education Digest 57 (6), 65–68.

Jalongo, M. (1995, Fall). Promoting active listening in the classroom. <u>Childhood Education, 72</u> (1), 13–18.

Kantrowitz, B. (1993, May 10). The group classroom: Why team learning may finally be catching on. <u>Newsweek, 121</u> (19), 73.

Kohn, A. (1993). <u>Punished by rewards: The trouble with gold stars, incentive plans, A's, praise, and other bribes.</u> New York: Houghton Mifflin.

Kohn, A. (1994, December). The truth about self-esteem. <u>Phi Delta Kappan, 76</u> (4), 272–283.

Kreidler W. (1995, November-December). Cultivating courtesy: Turning rude dudes into courteous kids. <u>Instructor 105</u> (4), 22–23.

Kreidler, W. (1996, January-February). Tell it like it is; how to ward off conflicts by improving kids' communication skills. <u>Instructor, 105</u> (5), 32–33.

Krucoff, C. (1995, July). Winning and losing: Learning to do both with grace boosts kids' self-esteem. <u>Parents Magazine, 70</u> (7), 43–44.

Lantieri, L., and Patti J. (1996, September). The road to peace in our schools. <u>Educational Leadership, 54</u> (1), 28–31.

Luke, J. and Myers, C. (1994, Winter). Toward peace: Using literature to aid conflict resolution. <u>Childhood Education, 71</u> (2) 66–69.

MacGregor, J. (1996, September). Poise 'n the hood: There's nothing wrong with America a little etiquette couldn't cure. <u>Los Angeles Magazine, 41</u> (9), 60–62.

Manning, M. L., and Lucking, R. (1993, September-October). Cooperative learning and multicultural classrooms. <u>The Clearing House, 67</u> (1), 12–16.

Marks, J. (1996, April). The American uncivil wars; how crude, rude and obnoxious behavior has replaced good manners and why that hurts our politics and power. <u>U.S. News & World Report, 120</u> (16), 66–72.

Maynard, J. (1995, March). Mind your manners. <u>Parenting, 9</u> (2), 49–50.

McCarthy, C. (1992, December 25). Needed: Teaching peace literacy by numbers. <u>National Catholic Reporter, 29</u> (9), 14.

McCormick, P. (1994, November). Mind your manners! <u>Parents Magazine, 69</u> (11), 48–50.

Moeller, T. (1994, January). What research says about self-esteem and academic performance. <u>Education Digest, 59</u> (5), 34–37.

Moran, V. (1992, September-October). Effective Communication. <u>The Animals' Agenda, 12</u> (7), 42–43.

Morse, P., and Andrea, R. (1994, October). Teaching kids to be peer mediators. <u>Education Digest, 60</u> (2), 53–56.

Muller, T. (1994, February). Exploring the facts about immigration. <u>The Chronicle of Higher Education, 40</u> (23), B1–2.

Murphy, C. (1994, May). A.K.A.: Is identity proliferation outstripping population growth? <u>The Atlantic Monthly, 73</u> (5), 26–27.

Murphy, T. (1994, September). Handicapping education. <u>National Review, 46</u> (17), 56–58.

Noriyuki, D. (1996, June 24). Heart and souls. <u>Los Angeles Times</u>, pages E1, E2.

Porro, B. (1996). Talk it out: Conflict resolution in the elementary classroom. Alexandria, VA: Association for Supervision and Curriculum Development.

Porter, K. (1992, May-June). Teaching peace. The Humanist, 52 (3), 32–33.

Power, J. (1992, May). One-stop help for kids. NEA Today, 10 (9), 25.

Pruffer, D. (1992, April). Playground peace talk. Parenting, 6 (3), 23.

Prutzman, P., et al. (1988). The friendly classroom for a small planet: A handbook on creative approaches to living and problem solving. Philadelphia: New Society Publishers.

Rich, D. (1992). MegaSkills. New York: Houghton Mifflin Company.

Ross, K. (Ed.). (1996, April). Through the years. Sesame Street Parents, 49–54.

Ryval, M. (1993, June). Nurturing individuality: It can boost your teen's self-esteem. Chatelaine, 66 (6), 22.

Saltzman, A. (1994, November). Schooled in failure? Fact or myth—teachers favor boys; girls respond by withdrawing. U.S. News & World Report, 117 (18), 88–92.

Seal, K. (1996, September). Unlock your child's potential. Family Circle, 109 (12), 77–81.

Seligman, M. (1995). The optimistic child. Boston: Houghton Mifflin.

Should school systems move toward "full inclusion"? (1993, December). CQ Researcher, 3 (46), 1,097.

Slavin, R. E. (1996, March-April). Cooperative learning in middle and secondary schools. The Clearing House, 69 (4) 200–204.

Smitherman, G. (1995, January). Students' right to their own language: A retrospective. English Journal, 84 (1), 21–27.

Spann, M. (1994, March). Make peace-keeping playful. Instructor, 103 (7), 24–25.

Spock, B. (1993, March). No contest! Parenting, 7 (2), 110–114.

Stevenson, H. (1996, January). Self-esteem: The myth of feeling good about oneself. USA Today Magazine, 124 (2608), 80–81.

Strommen, E. (1995, March). Cooperative learning: Technology may be the Trojan horse that brings collaboration into the classroom. Electronic Learning, 14 (6), 24–31.

Tsujimoto, J. (1993, January). Talk for the mind. English Journal, 82 (1), 34–37.

Webster's New World Dictionary (3rd ed.). (1994). New York: Simon & Schuster.

Weissbourd, R. (1996, August). The feel-good trap. The New Republic 215 (89), 12–14.

Welsch, R. (1994, March). The hyphenated American. Natural History, 103 (3), 24–25.

White, H. (1995, September 15). Never mind being innovative and effective—just be nice. Library Journal, 120 (15), 47–48.

W(h)ither full inclusion? (1995, January). Phi Delta Kappan, 76 (5), 415–417.

Wong, S. (1993, November). Beyond Bruce Lee. Essence 24 (7), 64–66.

Woolridge, V. (1993, March). Cooperative learning warm-ups: Spark a collaborative spirit in your classroom with these activities. Instructor, 102 (7), 49.